TAMPA

COMPREHENSIVE TRAVEL GUIDE 2025

Your Essential Pocket Guide for Exploring and Discovering Hidden Gems, Cultural Heritage, Culinary Delights, History, City Maps and Insider Tips of Tampa and its Neighborhoods

By

TIFFANY DOLAN

Copyright © 2025 Tiffany Dolan. All Rights Reserved. This publication, including all of its text, images, and associated content, is fully protected under international copyright laws. Any unauthorized reproduction, copying, distribution, or transmission of this material, whether in print, digital, or any other form, is strictly prohibited without prior written consent from the author. This includes sharing via electronic means, scanning, uploading, or redistribution on social media, websites, or other platforms.

Tiffany Dolan, a seasoned traveler and the author of numerous acclaimed travel guides, holds exclusive rights to this work. Any requests for permissions, whether for educational purposes, book clubs, presentations, or professional use, must be directed to the author through her author central page. In the request, please include specific details of the content you wish to use, as well as the purpose for which it is intended. All inquiries will be reviewed promptly, and the author will respond accordingly to grant or deny permission based on the proposed use. This copyright applies to the entirety of the publication and is intended to protect the intellectual property and creative efforts of the author. Legal action may be pursued against any individuals or entities found infringing upon these rights.

TABLE OF CONTENTS

Copyright.. 1
My Experience in Tampa.. 5
Benefits of this Guide.. 7

Chapter 1: Introduction to Tampa... 9
1.1 Welcome to Tampa... 9
1.2 History and Culture... 10
1.3 Geography and Climate.. 13
1.4 Getting Around Tampa.. 14
1.5 Tampa for First Time Travelers.. 16

Chapter 2: Accommodation Options... 18
2.1 Luxury Hotels and Resorts... 19
2.2 Budget-Friendly Options... 20
2.3 Vacation Rentals and Apartments... 21
2.4 Camping in Tampa.. 23
2.6 Boutique Hotels... 24
2.7 Unique Stays: Bed and Breakfasts.. 26

Chapter 3: Transportation.. 28
3.1 Getting to Tampa... 28
3.2 Public Transportation Options... 29
3.3 Car Rentals and Driving Tips... 30
3.4 Walking and Cycling Trails... 32
3.5 Shuttle Services.. 33

Chapter 4: Top 10 Attractions & Hidden Gems...................................... 35
4.1 Busch Gardens Tampa Bay... 36
4.2 Florida Aquarium.. 37
4.3 Lowry Park Zoo... 39

4.4 Museum of Science and Industry..41
4.5 Tampa Museum of Art...42
4.6 Henry B. Plant Museum..44
4.7 Ybor City Historic District..46
4.8 Tampa Riverwalk..48
4.9 Fort De Soto Park...50
4.10 Clearwater Beach...51
4.11 Outdoor Activities and Adventures...53
4.12 Guided Tours and Recommended Tour Operators....................54

Chapter 5 Practical Information and Guidance..................................56
5.1 Maps and Navigation...56
5.2 Three to Five Days Itinerary..59
5.3 Essential Packing List..60
5.4 Setting Your Travel Budget..63
5.5 Visa Requirements and Entry Procedures..................................65
5.6 Safety Tips and Emergency Contacts...66
5.7 Currency Exchange and Banking Services................................68
5.8 Language, Communication and Useful Phrases........................69
5.9 Shopping in Tampa..72
5.10 Health and Wellness Centers..74
5.11 Useful Websites, Mobile Apps and Online Resources..............76
5.12 Internet Access and Connectivity..77
5.13 Visitor Centers and Tourist Assistance......................................79

Chapter 6: Gastronomic Delights..81
6.1 Dining Options and Top Restaurants...81
6.2 Cafes and Bakeries..83
6.4 Cooking Classes and Culinary Tours..84
6.5 Traditional Floridian Cuisine..86
6.6 Local Markets and Street Food...87
6.7 Bars, Nightlife and Entertainment..89

Chapter 7: Day Trips and Excursions 91
7.1 St. Petersburg and the Gulf Coast 92
7.2 Clearwater and the Beaches 94
7.3 Sarasota and the Cultural Coast 95
7.4 Crystal River and the Nature Coast 97
7.5 Exploring Tampa's Neighboring Cities 98

Chapter 8: Events and Festivals 101
8.1 Gasparilla Pirate Festival 101
8.2 Tampa Bay Blues Festival 103
8.3 Florida Strawberry Festival 105
8.4 Tampa Bay Margarita Festival 107
8.5 Outback Bowl and College Football 109
Conclusion and Recommendations 112

MY EXPERIENCE IN TAMPA

The moment I stepped into Tampa, Florida, I felt an energy unlike any other. It wasn't just the sun casting golden reflections over the bay or the warm sea breeze that carried the scent of salt and adventure—it was something deeper, something alive. Tampa had a pulse, a rhythm, a character that instantly pulled me in. I had always heard about this vibrant city, often overshadowed by Florida's other hotspots like Miami and Orlando, but nothing could have prepared me for the magic that unfolded in front of me. Tampa is not just a destination; it is an experience, a journey through history, culture, and endless excitement. One of my first experiences in Tampa was standing at the edge of the Tampa Riverwalk, watching the Hillsborough River glisten under the afternoon sun. The Riverwalk is more than just a pathway—it is a living artery of the city, lined with parks, restaurants, and museums. As I strolled along, I found myself stopping every few minutes, captivated by the sights around me. Kayakers glided effortlessly through the calm waters, street performers filled the air with music, and locals jogged past, their smiles reflecting the easygoing spirit of the city. I followed the Riverwalk all the way to Armature Works, a historic warehouse turned into a lively food hall, where I savored fresh seafood and a perfectly crafted cocktail while soaking in the panoramic view of the city skyline.

Tampa, however, is not just about modern vibrancy—it is also a city of deep history. My curiosity led me to Ybor City, Tampa's historic Cuban district, where the scent of hand-rolled cigars and strong coffee drifted through the air. Walking through its cobblestone streets felt like stepping back in time. I watched as expert cigar makers crafted each piece by hand, their meticulous movements a reminder of the city's rich Cuban heritage. I sat at Columbia Restaurant, Florida's oldest restaurant, and indulged in a plate of their legendary 1905 Salad while sipping on sangria. The combination of Spanish flavors, the sound of live flamenco music, and the history embedded in the walls made the entire moment feel surreal. No trip to Tampa is complete without an encounter with its breathtaking coastline. The Gulf waters called my name, and I answered by spending a day at Clearwater Beach, a short drive from the city. The sand was so soft it felt like powdered sugar between my toes, and the turquoise waters stretched endlessly into the horizon. I took a deep breath, inhaling the salty ocean air, and let the waves wash away all my worries. I joined a sunset cruise, watching as the sky transformed into an explosion of pink, orange, and gold. At that moment, I understood why Tampa's sunsets were legendary—no camera could truly capture their magic.

Tampa's wildlife encounters were another highlight I never expected. At The Florida Aquarium, I found myself face-to-face with exotic marine creatures, from playful otters to majestic sharks gliding through the massive tanks. But nothing compared to the thrill of visiting ZooTampa at Lowry Park, where I had the chance to feed a giraffe and see a Florida panther up close. Tampa has a way of connecting you with nature in a way that feels personal, almost as if the city itself is inviting you to experience its wild, untamed beauty. As night fell, Tampa revealed yet another side of its personality—a vibrant, electric nightlife that I could not resist. Sparkman Wharf was the perfect place to unwind, with its waterfront views, craft beer, and live music. I danced under the neon lights, surrounded by a crowd of people who, like me, had fallen under Tampa's spell. The city had given me everything—a taste of history, a thrill of adventure, and moments of serenity by the sea. Leaving Tampa was harder than I expected. It had imprinted itself on me, in the way the sun kissed the skyline, in the flavors that lingered on my tongue, in the laughter that echoed through its streets. Tampa is not just a place to visit—it is a place to feel, to experience, to remember. And as I boarded my plane, looking down at the shimmering waters one last time, I knew this wasn't goodbye. Tampa had become a part of me, and I would return, again and again.

BENEFITS OF THIS GUIDE

Exploring Tampa, Florida, is an exciting experience filled with diverse attractions, stunning coastal views, and rich cultural heritage. This comprehensive guide is designed to provide visitors with everything they need to navigate the city effortlessly. From detailed maps to expert recommendations, this guide ensures a smooth and memorable trip.

Maps and Navigation: Understanding Tampa's layout is key to making the most of your visit, and this guide includes detailed maps of neighborhoods, transit routes, and top landmarks. It provides GPS-friendly navigation tips, ensuring travelers can easily find their way around. Whether by car, public transportation, or on foot, visitors will have the tools to move efficiently throughout the city.

Accommodation Options: Choosing the right place to stay is crucial, and this guide offers insights into luxury hotels, budget-friendly motels, and unique boutique stays. It includes information on amenities, locations, and proximity to major attractions, helping travelers make informed choices. Whether staying in downtown Tampa, Ybor City, or near the beach, visitors will find accommodations tailored to their preferences.

Transportation in Tampa: Navigating Tampa is effortless with the comprehensive breakdown of public transport options, rental services, and rideshares provided in this guide. It covers details about HART buses, TECO Line Streetcars, and water taxis, ensuring visitors can travel cost-effectively. Information on biking routes and pedestrian-friendly areas further enhances mobility throughout the city.

Top Attractions and Landmarks; Tampa is home to world-famous attractions, and this guide highlights must-visit spots such as Busch Gardens, The Florida Aquarium, and the Tampa Riverwalk. Each attraction is detailed with entry fees, best visiting times, and local tips for an enhanced experience. Whether travelers seek adventure, nature, or history, this guide covers the city's most iconic landmarks.

Practical Information and Travel Resources: For a hassle-free trip, this guide provides essential travel resources, emergency contacts, and local laws to help visitors stay informed. It includes weather patterns, currency exchange information, and safety tips to ensure a smooth experience. Updated insights on healthcare facilities and visitor assistance services make this guide an indispensable companion.

Culinary Delights: Food lovers will appreciate the guide's recommendations on Tampa's diverse culinary scene, from Cuban sandwiches to fresh seafood. It features top-rated restaurants, local street food spots, and hidden dining gems catering to all budgets. Visitors can explore trendy brunch cafés, fine-dining experiences, and family-friendly eateries with ease.

Culture and Heritage: Tampa's rich history is brought to life through its museums, historic districts, and vibrant arts scene covered in this guide. It explores Ybor City's Cuban influence, Native American heritage, and contemporary art spaces. Visitors can immerse themselves in theaters, cultural festivals, and historic landmarks that tell the story of Tampa's past and present.

Outdoor Activities and Adventures: For those who love the outdoors, this guide details beach destinations, water sports, and hiking trails perfect for adventure seekers. It includes insider tips on kayaking in Tampa Bay, exploring nature reserves, and taking sunset cruises. Whether looking for family-friendly parks or adrenaline-pumping excursions, this guide has something for every traveler.

Shopping in Tampa: Retail enthusiasts will find valuable insights into Tampa's best shopping districts, malls, and local markets. The guide covers high-end shopping at International Plaza, unique finds at Hyde Park Village, and bargain spots at local flea markets. Recommendations on souvenirs, artisan shops, and specialty stores help visitors take home a piece of Tampa.

Day Trips and Excursions: Beyond Tampa, this guide suggests exciting day trips to nearby destinations like St. Petersburg, Clearwater, and Sarasota. It provides details on transportation options, activities, and must-see sights for travelers wanting to explore beyond the city. From white sandy beaches to cultural hubs, visitors can enjoy a variety of nearby getaways.

Entertainment and Nightlife: For those looking for a vibrant nightlife scene, this guide covers Tampa's best bars, clubs, and live music venues. It includes rooftop bars with stunning views, beachside lounges, and energetic dance clubs for an unforgettable night out. Visitors can also find information on sports events, comedy shows, and entertainment hubs.

CHAPTER 1
INTRODUCTION TO TAMPA

1.1 Welcome to Tampa

Welcome to Tampa, a city where coastal beauty meets urban vibrance, offering a perfect blend of adventure, culture, and relaxation. Located on Florida's west coast along the stunning Gulf of Mexico, Tampa is a dynamic destination that welcomes travelers with its warm climate, picturesque waterfront, and diverse attractions. Whether you are visiting for the first time or returning to uncover more of its hidden gems, Tampa offers an unforgettable experience that caters to every type of traveler. From its historic districts to its modern entertainment hubs, this city thrives on a unique energy that blends rich history with contemporary innovation. For those arriving by air, Tampa International Airport provides seamless access to the city, with efficient transport options such as rental cars, ride-sharing services, and public transit to take you wherever you need to go. The city itself is well-connected, with an easy-to-navigate road system and a charming streetcar service that links key attractions in the downtown area. While Tampa is best explored with a mix of walking and driving, its layout ensures that whether you are venturing into the lively streets of Ybor City or enjoying a scenic drive along Bayshore Boulevard, getting around is both convenient and enjoyable.

Tampa's climate is one of its greatest appeals, offering sunshine almost year-round. Winters are mild, making it an ideal escape from colder regions, while summers are warm and inviting, perfect for enjoying the city's stunning beaches and waterfront activities. Whether you are here for thrilling amusement parks, rich cultural experiences, or simply to unwind by the bay, Tampa's diverse offerings ensure there is always something new to discover. The city is home to world-renowned attractions such as Busch Gardens, The Florida Aquarium, and ZooTampa, each providing unique experiences for visitors of all ages. Nature lovers will find endless opportunities to explore, from kayaking through the mangroves of the Hillsborough River to spotting dolphins in Tampa Bay. Food is an integral part of Tampa's identity, with a thriving culinary scene that reflects its multicultural heritage. Cuban influences are especially prominent, particularly in Ybor City, where visitors can enjoy a traditional Cuban sandwich or sip on rich, locally roasted coffee. The city's waterfront dining spots offer fresh seafood, while modern eateries and rooftop bars provide a taste of Tampa's evolving food culture. The nightlife is just as vibrant, with entertainment districts like Sparkman Wharf and SoHo buzzing with energy after sunset.

Culturally, Tampa is a city with a deep appreciation for art, music, and history. Museums such as the Tampa Bay History Center and the Salvador Dalí Museum in nearby St. Petersburg provide insight into the region's past and artistic contributions. Festivals and events fill the calendar year-round, from the lively Gasparilla Pirate Festival to the sophisticated Gasparilla Music and Arts Festival. The city embraces its heritage while continuously evolving, making every visit feel fresh and exciting. A first-time trip to Tampa is an invitation to experience Florida beyond the typical tourist destinations. It is a city that offers the best of both worlds—thrilling adventures and peaceful retreats, historic charm and modern indulgence, all wrapped in the warmth of its welcoming community. Whether you are here for a weekend getaway or an extended stay, Tampa has a way of making visitors feel at home while leaving them eager to return for more.

1.2 History and Culture
Tampa is a city where the past and present intertwine, offering visitors a rich tapestry of history and vibrant cultural influences. From its indigenous roots to

its diverse immigrant communities, the city has evolved into a dynamic destination that reflects the spirit of its people.

The Indigenous and Early Settlers: Long before Tampa became a thriving metropolis, it was home to the Tocobaga people, who lived along the bay's shores and thrived on fishing and trade. Their civilization left behind shell mounds and artifacts that provide insight into their way of life. Spanish explorers arrived in the 16th century, bringing dramatic changes to the region through their encounters with indigenous tribes. While early European attempts at colonization failed, the area's strategic location made it a point of interest for future settlers.

The Rise of Tampa as a Port City: In the 19th century, Tampa's transformation began with the establishment of Fort Brooke, a military outpost that laid the foundation for the city's expansion. The arrival of the railroad in the late 1800s connected Tampa to the rest of the country, accelerating its growth. The city became a key hub for shipping and trade, with goods flowing in and out of its bustling port. The discovery of phosphate deposits further strengthened its economy, leading to rapid industrialization and new waves of migration.

The Cuban, Spanish, and Italian Influence: Tampa's cultural heart beats strongest in Ybor City, a historic neighborhood that became the center of cigar manufacturing in the late 1800s. Immigrants from Cuba, Spain, and Italy arrived in search of opportunities, bringing their languages, customs, and traditions. Cuban cigar factories flourished, and the area became known as the "Cigar Capital of the World." Today, visitors can still witness the legacy of this era through historic cigar shops, authentic Latin cuisine, and vibrant street festivals.

The Latin Flavor of Tampa: Tampa's Latino heritage is deeply ingrained in its identity, from the rhythmic beats of salsa music to the aroma of Cuban sandwiches that fill the streets. Cafés serve strong Cuban coffee, known as café con leche, and bakeries offer pastelitos filled with guava and cream cheese. Each year, the city celebrates its Latin roots with events like the Festa Italiana and the Ybor City Cigar Heritage Festival, keeping traditions alive for future generations.

The Pirate Legacy and Gasparilla Festival: One of Tampa's most famous cultural events is Gasparilla, an annual pirate-themed festival that takes over the city every January. Inspired by the legend of José Gaspar, a Spanish pirate who allegedly roamed Florida's coast, the festival brings elaborate parades, flotillas, and street celebrations. Locals and visitors dress as pirates, tossing beads and reveling in the lively atmosphere. The event is a spectacle of music, costumes, and performances, making it one of the most anticipated celebrations in Florida.

The Growth of Arts and Theater: Tampa is home to a thriving arts and theater scene, with venues like the Tampa Theatre and the Straz Center for the Performing Arts showcasing world-class performances. The city's museums, such as the Tampa Museum of Art and the Henry B. Plant Museum, provide insights into its artistic and historical legacy. Murals and street art line the walls of districts like Seminole Heights, where creativity and self-expression flourish.

A City of Sports and Traditions: Tampa's culture is also deeply connected to sports, with passionate fans supporting teams like the Tampa Bay Buccaneers, Tampa Bay Lightning, and Tampa Bay Rays. The city has hosted multiple Super Bowls, bringing global attention to its vibrant sports culture. Whether cheering at Raymond James Stadium or watching a hockey game at Amalie Arena, the excitement of Tampa's sports scene is contagious.

A Tapestry of Cultures in Modern Tampa: Today, Tampa is a melting pot where different cultures coexist, creating a city that is diverse and welcoming. Caribbean influences blend with Southern traditions, and European legacies remain alive in historic architecture and culinary delights. Festivals celebrating Greek, African, and Asian cultures bring together people from all backgrounds, making Tampa a true representation of global heritage.

Experiencing Tampa's History and Culture: For visitors, exploring Tampa's history and culture is a journey that can be experienced through its landmarks, food, music, and people. Walking through the cobblestone streets of Ybor City, tasting freshly rolled cigars, or witnessing a flamenco performance at the Columbia Restaurant offers a glimpse into the city's soul. Every corner of Tampa tells a story, inviting travelers to become part of its ever-evolving narrative.

A Timeless Destination for All: Tampa is not just a city; it is a living museum of history, a cultural crossroads, and a celebration of traditions that continue to thrive. Whether visiting for its past or its present, travelers will find themselves immersed in an experience unlike any other. It is a place where heritage is honored, diversity is embraced, and every street holds a story waiting to be discovered.

1.3 Geography and Climate

Tampa is a city where land meets water in the most stunning way, creating a landscape that is both captivating and diverse. Positioned on Florida's Gulf Coast, this vibrant city is surrounded by scenic bay waters, lush wetlands, and picturesque islands. It is located on the western side of the Florida Peninsula, bordered by Tampa Bay, a vast estuary that flows into the Gulf of Mexico. The unique geography of Tampa not only enhances its natural beauty but also influences its weather patterns, making it a destination that thrives on sunshine and outdoor adventures.

The Coastal and Urban Landscape: Tampa's geography is a mesmerizing blend of urban development, coastal marshes, and green spaces, giving visitors the best of both city life and natural retreats. The downtown area sits along the Hillsborough River, offering waterfront parks, modern skyscrapers, and bustling cultural districts. To the west, Tampa Bay stretches toward the Gulf, where mangrove forests, barrier islands, and white-sand beaches form an intricate coastal ecosystem. The city's layout is defined by its waterways, with scenic bridges and boardwalks that connect neighborhoods and provide endless opportunities for exploration.

Tropical Climate and Year-Round Sunshine: Tampa enjoys a humid subtropical climate, which means visitors can expect warm temperatures and sunshine throughout most of the year. Summers are long, hot, and humid, with daytime temperatures averaging around 90°F (32°C), while evenings bring cooling breezes from the bay. Winters are mild and pleasant, with daytime highs often reaching 70°F (21°C), making Tampa a perfect escape for those looking to avoid harsh northern winters. Spring and fall offer the best balance of warmth and comfortable humidity, making these seasons ideal for outdoor activities.

Seasonal Changes and Weather Patterns: Despite its generally sunny reputation, Tampa's climate follows distinct seasonal shifts that travelers should consider when planning their visit. Summer and early fall bring the wet season, characterized by frequent afternoon thunderstorms that roll in quickly and leave just as fast. Winter and spring are drier, with lower humidity and clearer skies, making them the best times for sightseeing, beach outings, and exploring the city. Due to its coastal location, Tampa is also prone to occasional hurricanes during the Atlantic hurricane season, which runs from June to November.

The Influence of Tampa Bay on the Climate: Tampa's proximity to the bay and the Gulf of Mexico plays a significant role in shaping its climate and weather. The waters surrounding the city help moderate temperatures, preventing extreme heat waves in summer and keeping winters mild. The sea breezes from the Gulf provide a cooling effect, making even the hottest days feel more bearable. The bay also supports a rich marine ecosystem, with abundant wildlife, including dolphins, manatees, and various bird species. Visitors can experience this firsthand through boat tours, kayaking, and waterfront dining with panoramic views of the bay.

The Best Time to Visit Tampa: Choosing when to visit Tampa depends on the kind of experience travelers seek, as each season offers something unique. Winter and early spring, from December to April, are the most popular months, with sunny days and mild temperatures that make exploring the city a delight. Summer, from June to September, is best for beach lovers and festival-goers, though travelers should be prepared for occasional rain showers. Fall, from October to November, brings slightly cooler temperatures and fewer crowds, making it a great time for a quieter, more relaxed visit.

A City Defined by Nature and Climate: Tampa's geography and climate create a perfect balance between urban sophistication and coastal beauty, offering visitors a setting that is both dynamic and inviting. Whether strolling along the Riverwalk, watching the sun set over Tampa Bay, or feeling the soft gulf breezes at a beachfront café, the city's natural elements shape every experience. The combination of tropical warmth, diverse landscapes, and year-round sunshine ensures that no matter when visitors arrive, Tampa welcomes them with open arms and endless possibilities for adventure.

1.4 Getting Around Tampa

Tampa is a city that blends modern infrastructure with historic charm, offering visitors multiple ways to explore its vibrant neighborhoods and scenic waterfront. Whether traveling by car, public transit, or on foot, getting around Tampa is an experience in itself, revealing the city's energy and diverse landscapes.

Driving and Car Rentals: For those who prefer flexibility, renting a car is one of the most convenient ways to navigate Tampa's sprawling layout. The city's well-maintained highways, including Interstate 275 and the Selmon Expressway, provide smooth connections between downtown, the beaches, and surrounding attractions. Parking is generally easy to find, with garages and metered spots available in major districts like Ybor City and the Riverwalk area. While traffic can be heavy during rush hours, driving allows visitors to explore beyond the city, including trips to Clearwater Beach and St. Petersburg.

The Tampa Streetcar: The TECO Line Streetcar System is a charming way to travel between downtown Tampa, the Channel District, and Ybor City. These vintage-style streetcars offer a nostalgic journey through the city's historic core, providing both convenience and a glimpse into Tampa's past. The streetcar is free to ride and operates daily, making it a budget-friendly and scenic mode of transport. Riding through Ybor City at night is particularly magical, as the district's neon lights and brick-lined streets come alive with energy.

Public Buses and Local Transit: Tampa's HART (Hillsborough Area Regional Transit) bus system connects key parts of the city, offering an affordable option for visitors who prefer public transport. Buses run frequently along major routes, serving destinations like the Tampa International Airport, Busch Gardens, and University of South Florida. The In-Towner Downtown Shuttle is another free service that loops through downtown Tampa, making it easy to reach business hubs, cultural attractions, and shopping districts without the need for a car.

Water Taxis and Ferries: Tampa's location along the Hillsborough River makes water transportation both scenic and practical. The Pirate Water Taxi offers a unique way to see the city while making stops at major attractions like Armature Works, the Convention Center, and the Florida Aquarium. Passengers can hop on and off throughout the day, enjoying stunning waterfront views and a relaxing alternative to road travel. For those wanting to venture to the beaches, the Cross Bay Ferry provides a direct connection between downtown Tampa and St. Petersburg, offering a smooth ride across the bay.

Biking and Walking Along the Riverwalk: The Tampa Riverwalk is a pedestrian-friendly path that stretches along the waterfront, connecting parks, museums, and restaurants. Walking or biking along this route is one of the best ways to experience the city's vibrant atmosphere while taking in views of the

Hillsborough River. Bike rentals and electric scooters are widely available throughout downtown, allowing visitors to explore at their own pace. Whether taking a morning jog or enjoying a sunset stroll, the Riverwalk offers a peaceful escape from the hustle and bustle of city life.

Rideshares and Taxis: For those needing quick and convenient transport, rideshare services like Uber and Lyft operate throughout Tampa, providing easy access to any destination. Traditional taxis are also available at major hubs such as the airport, cruise terminals, and downtown hotels. Whether heading to a nightlife district or catching an early morning flight, rideshares offer a hassle-free way to move around the city.

A City Built for Exploration: Tampa's transportation network is designed to accommodate every type of traveler, making it easy to discover the city's hidden gems. From vintage streetcars to modern ferries, every mode of transit offers a unique perspective of Tampa's charm. Whether cruising along the Riverwalk, taking a scenic streetcar ride, or driving along coastal highways, getting around Tampa is as much a part of the adventure as the destination itself.

1.5 Tampa for First Time Travelers
Tampa welcomes first-time visitors with its irresistible mix of sun-drenched coastlines, lively urban neighborhoods, and a rich cultural history. This Florida gem is more than just a stopover; it is an experience waiting to unfold, offering adventure, relaxation, and a taste of the tropics in one dynamic city. Whether you arrive with an itinerary in mind or prefer to let Tampa surprise you, the city offers countless ways to make your visit unforgettable. From its historic streets to its modern waterfront attractions, every corner of Tampa has something special to offer.

Arriving in Tampa and Getting Around: Stepping off the plane at Tampa International Airport, visitors are greeted with a smooth and efficient travel experience. The airport is known for its user-friendly layout, making navigation effortless even for those arriving for the first time. Transportation into the city is easy, with rental cars, ride-sharing services, and public transportation readily available. Tampa is a city best explored with a mix of driving and walking, as many attractions are spread out, but downtown areas are pedestrian-friendly. The TECO Streetcar System is a free and fun way to travel between downtown, Channelside, and the historic district of Ybor City.

Exploring the Best of Tampa's Neighborhoods: Each neighborhood in Tampa offers a distinct atmosphere, giving first-time travelers a variety of experiences to explore. Downtown Tampa is home to modern high-rises, waterfront parks, and cultural landmarks like the Tampa Museum of Art and the Straz Center for the Performing Arts. Ybor City, the city's historic Cuban district, transports visitors to another era with its vintage brick streets, cigar shops, and vibrant nightlife. The Riverwalk, stretching along the Hillsborough River, is a must-see, lined with restaurants, museums, and scenic views perfect for a leisurely stroll.

The Best Attractions to Experience: First-time visitors will find a mix of thrilling attractions and serene escapes, making it easy to tailor the perfect itinerary. Busch Gardens Tampa Bay is a must for adventure seekers, offering world-class roller coasters, exotic animal encounters, and thrilling safari tours. The Florida Aquarium provides an immersive marine life experience, perfect for families and nature lovers alike. Those looking for outdoor beauty should explore Bayshore Boulevard, a scenic waterfront path that showcases stunning views of the bay and the downtown skyline.

Tampa's Culinary Scene and Local Favorites: First-time travelers will quickly realize that Tampa is a food lover's paradise, with flavors influenced by Cuban, Spanish, and Southern traditions. A visit to Columbia Restaurant, Florida's oldest Spanish restaurant, is a must for those wanting to taste Tampa's rich culinary heritage. The Cuban sandwich, a local staple, can be found in many eateries, but the best versions are in Ybor City, where the dish originated. Seafood lovers can indulge in fresh Gulf catches at waterfront restaurants, while those seeking casual bites will enjoy Tampa's booming food truck scene.

Tampa's Beaches and Coastal Escapes: No visit to Tampa is complete without experiencing its stunning nearby beaches, which offer the perfect escape from the city's energy. Clearwater Beach, just a short drive away, boasts powdery white sand and crystal-clear waters, perfect for a day of relaxation. St. Pete Beach, known for its laid-back charm, offers breathtaking sunsets and a lively boardwalk scene. Many visitors choose to take a sunset cruise or rent a kayak to explore the bay's tranquil waters, where dolphins and manatees are often spotted.

Entertainment, Nightlife, and Events: As the sun sets, Tampa transforms into a city filled with nightlife, entertainment, and cultural events. Sparkman Wharf, a lively waterfront destination, is the perfect spot for evening cocktails, live music, and socializing. For those seeking a more energetic scene, SoHo (South Howard Avenue) is the go-to area for trendy bars, nightclubs, and rooftop lounges. Sports fans can catch a Tampa Bay Lightning hockey game or watch the Tampa Bay Buccaneers in action, immersing themselves in the city's passionate sports culture.

CHAPTER 2
ACCOMMODATION OPTIONS

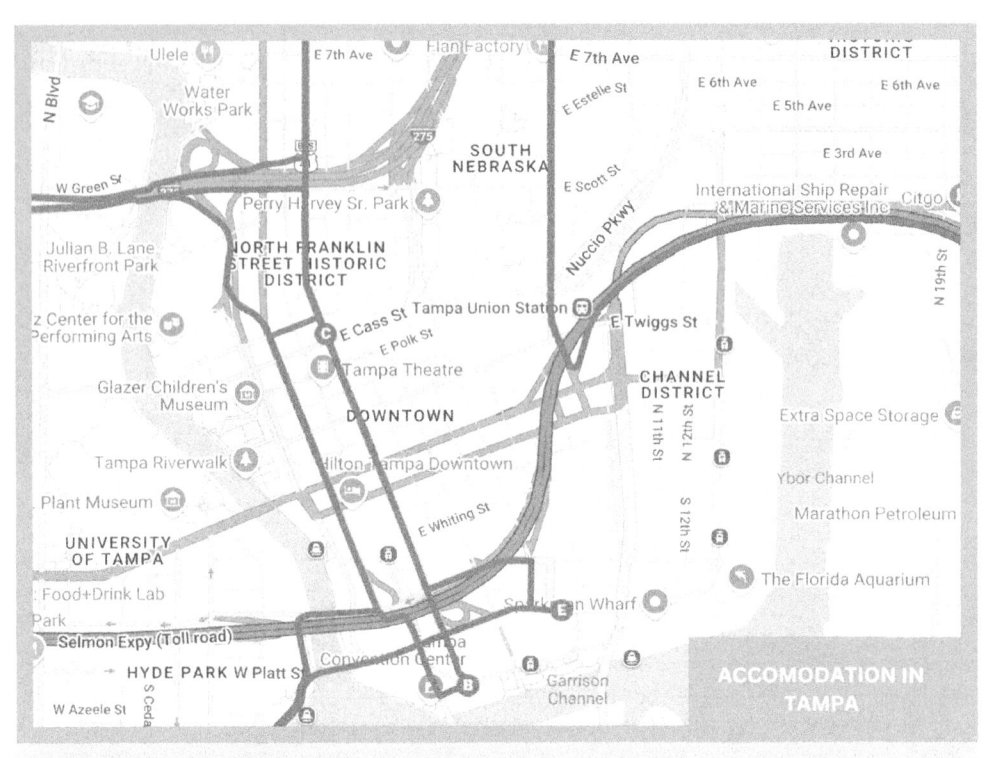

ACCOMODATION IN TAMPA

Directions from Tampa International Airport (TPA), George J Bean Parkway, Tampa, FL, USA
Spark by Hilton Tampa Brandon, Horace Avenue, Tampa, FL, USA

A
Tampa International Airport, (TPA), George J Bean Parkway, Tampa, FL, USA

B
JW Marriott Tampa Water Street, Water Street, Tampa, FL, USA

C
Hotel Flor Tampa Downtown, Tapestry Collection by Hilton. North Florida Avenue, Tampa, FL, USA

D
Epicurean Hotel. Autograph Collection, South Howard Avenue, Tampa, FL, USA

E
The Tampa EDITION, Channelside Drive, Tampa, FL, USA

F
Grand Hyatt Tampa Bay, Bayport Drive, Tampa, FL, USA

G
Palm Villa Hostel's, East Palm Avenue, Tampa, FL, USA

H
Red Roof Inn Tampa - Brandon, Horace Avenue. Tampa, FL, USA

I
Spark by Hilton Tampa Brandon, Horace Avenue, Tampa FL, USA

2.1 Luxury Hotels and Resorts

Tampa, Florida, offers a selection of luxury accommodations that cater to travelers seeking exceptional comfort and service. Each hotel provides unique experiences, ensuring a memorable stay in this vibrant city.

JW Marriott Tampa Water Street: Located in the heart of downtown at 510 Water Street, the JW Marriott Tampa Water Street offers elegantly designed rooms with city and water views. Guests can enjoy a variety of dining options, including signature restaurants and a rooftop bar. Amenities include a full-service spa, fitness center, and an outdoor pool. Room rates start at approximately $350 per night. For reservations, visit www.marriott.com/en-us/hotels/tpajd-jw-marriott-tampa-water-street/overview/.

Hotel Flor Tampa: Combining historic charm with modern luxury, Hotel Flor Tampa is situated at 905 North Florida Avenue. The hotel features elegantly appointed rooms and suites, a speakeasy-inspired restaurant called The Dan, and the Cass Street Coffee Company for light fare. Amenities include a fitness center and event spaces. Room rates begin around $250 per night. More information and bookings are available at www.hotelflortampa.com/.

Epicurean Hotel, Autograph Collection: Located in the trendy SoHo district at 1207 South Howard Avenue, the Epicurean Hotel is a haven for food enthusiasts. The hotel boasts 137 guest rooms designed with culinary-inspired décor, a rooftop bar, and the renowned Élevage SoHo Kitchen & Bar. Amenities include a full-service spa, culinary classroom, and an outdoor pool. Rates start at approximately $300 per night. Reservations can be made through www.epicureanhotel.com/.

The Tampa EDITION: Situated within the Water Street Tampa neighborhood at 500 Channelside Drive, The Tampa EDITION offers 172 guest rooms and suites with modern design elements. The hotel features seven food and beverage venues, including a signature restaurant and a rooftop bar with a terrace. Additional amenities include an expansive spa, fitness center, and over 550 square meters of flexible meeting and event space. Room rates begin at around $400 per night. For more details, visit www.editionhotels.com/tampa/.

Grand Hyatt Tampa Bay: Set on a 35-acre wildlife preserve at 2900 Bayport Drive, the Grand Hyatt Tampa Bay provides a resort-like experience with city convenience. The hotel offers 442 guest rooms, including casitas located amid the natural landscape. Amenities feature two outdoor pools, a 24-hour fitness center, and multiple dining options, such as the award-winning Oystercatchers restaurant. Room rates start at approximately $250 per night. Each of these luxury hotels in Tampa provides distinct experiences, ensuring that visitors can find the perfect accommodation to suit their preferences and enhance their stay in this dynamic city.

2.2 Budget-Friendly Options

Traveling to Tampa on a budget doesn't mean compromising on comfort or convenience. The city offers a variety of affordable accommodations that provide excellent amenities and unique features, ensuring a pleasant stay for every traveler. Here are some notable options to consider:

Palm Villa Hostel: Located in the heart of Tampa, Palm Villa Hostel offers budget-conscious travelers a cozy and friendly environment. With dorm beds starting at approximately $34 per night, it stands as one of the most affordable options in the city. Guests can enjoy communal spaces, free Wi-Fi, and a shared kitchen, fostering a social atmosphere ideal for meeting fellow travelers. Its proximity to public transportation makes exploring Tampa's attractions convenient and hassle-free. For further inquiries and reservations, log on to their website.

Red Roof Inn Tampa - Brandon; Situated at 10121 Horace Avenue, Red Roof Inn Tampa - Brandon provides affordable lodging without sacrificing quality. The hotel offers comfortable rooms equipped with modern amenities, including free Wi-Fi and flat-screen TVs. Guests can take advantage of the outdoor pool and complimentary parking. Its location near major highways allows easy access to downtown Tampa and nearby attractions. Bookings and reservations are available on their website.

Spark by Hilton Tampa Brandon: Located at 10110 Horace Avenue, Spark by Hilton Tampa Brandon offers budget-friendly accommodations with the reliability of the Hilton brand. The hotel features well-appointed rooms, a fitness center, and complimentary breakfast to start your day. With rates that cater to budget travelers, it provides excellent value for money. Its convenient location near shopping centers and restaurants adds to its appeal. More details and reservations are available on their website.

Holiday Inn - Tampa North, an IHG Hotel: Positioned at 3751 E. Fowler Ave, Holiday Inn - Tampa North offers affordable rates with the comfort and service associated with the IHG brand. The hotel features spacious rooms, an outdoor pool, and an on-site restaurant. Guests can enjoy free Wi-Fi and a complimentary shuttle service to nearby attractions, including the University of South Florida and Busch Gardens. For booking information, visit their website.

Hotel in Express Tampa- Rocky Point Island, an IHG Hotel: Located at 3025 North Rocky Point Drive, this Holiday Inn Express provides budget-friendly accommodations with scenic views of the bay. The hotel offers modern rooms, a fitness center, and a complimentary breakfast bar. Its location near the airport and major attractions makes it a convenient choice for travelers. For reservations, visit their website.

Holiday Inn Express Tampa-Rocky Point Island, an IHG Hotel: Located at 8610 Elm Fair Boulevard, this hotel offers affordable lodging with easy access to the Florida State Fairgrounds and the Seminole Hard Rock Casino. Guests can enjoy amenities such as an outdoor pool, free Wi-Fi, and a complimentary hot breakfast. The spacious rooms and friendly service make it a popular choice among budget travelers. To get more information on pricing and reservations, visit their website. Each of these accommodations provides a unique blend of comfort, convenience, and affordability, ensuring that budget-conscious travelers can enjoy all that Tampa has to offer without breaking the bank.

2.3 Vacation Rentals and Apartments

Exploring Tampa's vibrant culture and scenic beauty becomes even more enjoyable when staying in accommodations that offer the comforts of home. Vacation rentals and apartments provide flexibility, space, and a personalized experience, allowing visitors to immerse themselves fully in the local atmosphere. Here are some notable options in Tampa

Florida Sun Vacation Rentals: Florida Sun Vacation Rentals offers a selection of luxury homes in prime locations around Tampa, including properties on the water or near world-class beaches. Each rental is thoughtfully equipped with plush bedding, beach toys, bicycles, and heated swimming pools, ensuring a comfortable and enjoyable stay. Guests can easily access nearby attractions such as golf courses, hiking trails, amusement parks, tennis courts, and theaters. The company provides personalized guidance to match travelers with the perfect home, enhancing the overall vacation experience. For further enquiry and reservations log on to their official site floridasunvacationrentals.com

Vacasa Vacation Rentals: Vacasa professionally manages a wide array of vacation rentals across Tampa, ensuring each home meets high standards of comfort and cleanliness. From family-friendly resort condos with pools to luxurious beachfront villas, Vacasa offers accommodations to suit various preferences. Guests can enjoy amenities such as private pools, hot tubs, and proximity to local attractions. The company's commitment to quality and service makes it a reliable choice for travelers seeking a home-away-from-home experience.

Resort Rentals: Specializing in vacation condos along St. Pete Beach and surrounding areas, Resort Rentals provides properties either on the beach or the bay, offering stunning waterfront views. These fully equipped condos, homes, and villas come with amenities like full kitchens, spacious living areas, and access to community pools. Their locations offer easy access to Tampa's attractions, making them a convenient choice for visitors looking to explore both the city and the coast.

Airbnb Tampa Condo Rentals: Airbnb offers a variety of condo rentals in Tampa, catering to different budgets and preferences. Options range from cozy studios to spacious multi-bedroom units, many featuring amenities such as pools, hot tubs, and pet-friendly policies. Staying in an Airbnb allows travelers to experience Tampa like a local, with properties often situated in residential neighborhoods close to dining, shopping, and entertainment venues. To get more insight and reservations , visit their website: airbnb.com

FloridaRentals.com: FloridaRentals.com lists a wide selection of vacation homes for rent by owner in Tampa and the surrounding areas. Properties range from beachfront houses to downtown condos, each offering unique features and amenities. Many rentals come with private pools, fully equipped kitchens, and spacious outdoor areas, providing a comfortable and private retreat for travelers. Booking through FloridaRentals.com connects guests directly with property owners, often resulting in cost savings and personalized service.More Informations and reservations are available on their website: floridarentals.com

HomeToGo Vacation Rentals: HomeToGo aggregates vacation rental listings from various providers, offering an extensive selection of cabins, condos, houses, and other accommodations in Tampa. The platform allows travelers to compare prices and amenities across different properties, ensuring they find the perfect rental to suit their needs. With options ranging from budget-friendly apartments to luxury villas, HomeToGo caters to a wide range of preferences and budgets. For further information and bookings, visit their website: hometogo.com Each of these options provides a unique experience, allowing visitors to choose accommodations that best fit their preferences and enhance their stay in Tampa.

2.4 Camping in Tampa

Tampa, Florida, offers a variety of camping experiences that cater to both nature enthusiasts and those seeking modern amenities. From state parks showcasing Florida's natural beauty to resorts providing luxury accommodations, campers can find the perfect spot to enjoy the outdoors.

Hillsborough River State Park: Located just minutes from downtown Tampa at 15402 U.S. 301 North, Thonotosassa, Hillsborough River State Park offers a serene escape into nature. The park features over seven miles of nature trails, providing ample opportunities for wildlife viewing and hiking. Campers can choose from 112 sites equipped with water, electric hookups, a fire ring, and a picnic table. Restrooms in each loop offer hot showers and laundry facilities for added comfort. The park also offers canoe and kayak rentals for those looking to explore the Class II river rapids. Reservations can be made up to 11 months in advance through the Florida State Parks reservation system.

E.G. Simmons County Park: Situated at 2401 19th Avenue NW in Ruskin, E.G. Simmons County Park spans 469 acres along Tampa Bay. The park boasts 103 campsites, most of which are waterfront, offering picturesque views. Each site includes a fire ring, picnic table, water, and electric hookups, with dump stations nearby. Visitors can enjoy activities such as kayaking, canoeing, and fishing in the park's numerous waterways. The park's natural setting provides a tranquil camping experience close to the city.

Camp Margaritaville RV Resort Auburndale: Located at 361 Denton Avenue in Auburndale, Camp Margaritaville RV Resort offers a blend of luxury and adventure. The resort features 326 RV sites, including 11 Super Premium sites, and 75 Cabana Cabins for those without RVs. Amenities include resort pools, a tiki bar, fire pits, a playground, dog parks, and a putting course. Its central location between Tampa and Orlando makes it an ideal base for exploring Central Florida's attractions. Reservations and more information are available on their website.

MacDill Air Force Base FamCamp: Exclusively for military personnel and their families, MacDill AFB FamCamp is located within the base in Tampa. The campground operates year-round, offering 359 full-service sites equipped with electricity, water, waste disposal, cable TV, and optional telephone service. Additional facilities include 41 dry camp sites, 21 partial hook-up spots, and a tent camping area. The FamCamp provides a secure and well-maintained environment for military campers.

St. Petersburg / Madeira Beach KOA Holiday: Situated at 5400 95th Street North in St. Petersburg, this KOA campground offers a variety of camping options, including tent sites, RV sites, and cabin rentals. Amenities feature a heated pool, hot tub, mini-golf, and bike rentals. The campground is located near the Pinellas Trail, providing easy access to miles of scenic biking and walking paths. Its proximity to Gulf Coast beaches makes it a popular choice for campers looking to enjoy both outdoor activities and beach relaxation.

Clearwater / Lake Tarpon KOA Holiday: Located at 37061 US Hwy 19 N in Palm Harbor, this KOA offers a peaceful setting near Lake Tarpon. The campground provides full-hookup RV sites, tent sites, and cabin accommodations. Amenities include a swimming pool, fishing dock, and a Kamp K9® dog park for pets. Its location offers easy access to nearby attractions such as the Tarpon Springs Sponge Docks and the beaches of Clearwater. Reservations can be made through their website. Each of these camping destinations near Tampa provides unique experiences, from immersing oneself in Florida's natural landscapes to enjoying resort-style amenities. Whether seeking a rustic retreat or a luxurious getaway, campers can find the perfect spot to suit their preferences.

2.6 Boutique Hotels

Tampa's boutique hotels offer a unique blend of luxury, history, and personalized service, providing travelers with memorable experiences that reflect the city's vibrant culture. Here are five exceptional boutique hotels in Tampa, each with its own distinctive charm.

Hotel Haya: Located in the heart of Ybor City, Hotel Haya captures the essence of Tampa's historic Latin Quarter. This boutique hotel seamlessly blends old-world charm with modern amenities, offering guests a unique experience. The hotel's design pays homage to the area's rich cultural heritage, featuring vibrant decor and thoughtful details. Guests can enjoy amenities such as an on-site restaurant, a lively bar, and a courtyard pool. Its prime location provides easy access to Ybor City's eclectic mix of shops, restaurants, and nightlife. For reservations and more information, visit their official website: https://hotelhaya.com/.

Palihouse Hyde Park Village: Situated in Tampa's historic Hyde Park neighborhood, Palihouse Hyde Park Village offers residential-inspired suites that provide a home-away-from-home experience. The hotel's 36 oversized guest rooms are designed with bespoke furnishings, creating a cozy yet sophisticated atmosphere. Guests can unwind in the intimate lobby lounge and cocktail bar or explore the tree-lined streets of Hyde Park, known for its stately homes and 19th-century architecture. The hotel's proximity to local boutiques and eateries makes it an ideal choice for travelers seeking a blend of comfort and convenience. For bookings and additional details, visit: https://www.palisociety.com/hotels/tampa.

Epicurean Hotel, Autograph Collection: Located in the trendy SoHo district, the Epicurean Hotel is a haven for food and wine enthusiasts. This AAA Four Diamond hotel features 137 guest rooms and suites, each thoughtfully designed to reflect a culinary theme. Amenities include a state-of-the-art culinary classroom, a full-service spa, and a rooftop bar offering panoramic views of the city. The on-site restaurant serves delectable dishes that celebrate local flavors, making it a destination in itself. With its focus on gastronomy and luxury, the Epicurean Hotel provides a feast for the senses. To learn more or make a reservation, visit: https://www.epicureanhotel.com/.

Le Méridien Tampa, The Courthouse: Housed in a century-old federal courthouse, Le Méridien Tampa offers a unique blend of historic architecture and modern design. The hotel's 130 guest rooms feature contemporary furnishings while preserving elements of the building's storied past, such as original oak doors and terrazzo flooring. Amenities include an outdoor pool, a fitness center, and an on-site French-inspired restaurant. Its downtown location provides easy access to Tampa's cultural attractions, including museums, theaters, and the Riverwalk. For travelers seeking a stay that combines history with luxury, Le Méridien Tampa is an excellent choice. More information and reservations are available at: https://www.marriott.com/hotels/travel/tpamd-le-meridien-tampa/.

Hotel Flor: Embracing its 1920s art deco heritage, Hotel Flor offers guests a blend of historic charm and modern luxury. Located in downtown Tampa, the hotel features elegantly appointed rooms with contemporary amenities to ensure a comfortable stay. Guests can indulge in exquisite dining at the on-site restaurant, which offers a menu that fuses classic and modern culinary delights. The hotel's prime location makes it a convenient base for exploring Tampa's attractions, including the nearby Riverwalk and cultural venues. For those interested in a stay that reflects Tampa's rich history while providing modern comforts, Hotel Flor is an ideal choice. For bookings and further details, visit: https://www.hotelflortampa.com/. Each of these boutique hotels offers a distinct experience, allowing travelers to immerse themselves in Tampa's unique culture and history while enjoying exceptional accommodations.

2.7 Unique Stays: Bed and Breakfasts

Tampa, Florida, offers a variety of unique bed and breakfast accommodations that provide personalized experiences for travelers seeking a more intimate stay. Each establishment reflects the city's diverse culture and history, ensuring guests enjoy a memorable visit.

Phantom History House: Located in the Citrus Park area of Tampa, Phantom History House offers themed guest rooms that blend modern comfort with a touch of the supernatural. Each room is uniquely decorated, providing an immersive experience for guests. Amenities include complimentary breakfast, Wi-Fi, and access to common areas designed for relaxation and socializing. Room rates start at approximately $185 per night. Further Informations and reservations are available on their website

Gram's Place Bed and Hostel: Situated in Tampa Heights, Gram's Place is a music-themed bed and breakfast that celebrates various genres and artists. The establishment offers both private rooms and shared hostel accommodations, catering to a diverse range of travelers. Guests can enjoy amenities such as a hot tub, rooftop deck, and communal kitchen. The eclectic decor and vibrant atmosphere make it a favorite among those seeking a creative and communal lodging experience. Prices vary depending on the type of accommodation selected.

The Pickett Fence: Located in the historic district of Plant City, just a short drive from Tampa, The Pickett Fence provides a quaint and charming retreat. This bed and breakfast features cozy rooms adorned with antique furnishings, reflecting the area's rich history. Guests are treated to homemade breakfasts and can enjoy the serene garden spaces on the property. The warm hospitality and peaceful environment offer a relaxing getaway. Room rates and availability can be found on their website.

Tampa Heights Bungalow - Bed & Breakfast: Located in the heart of Tampa Heights, this bungalow-style bed and breakfast offers guests a blend of historic charm and modern amenities. The property features well-appointed rooms, each with its own unique decor. Guests can enjoy a homemade breakfast each morning and relax in the cozy common areas or on the inviting porch. Its proximity to downtown Tampa makes it a convenient choice for travelers looking to explore the city's attractions. Room rates start at approximately $120 per night.

Palmetto Riverside Bed and Breakfast: Situated along the Manatee River in Palmetto, a short drive from Tampa, this historic inn offers elegant accommodations with scenic river views. The property boasts beautifully landscaped gardens, a grand veranda, and tastefully decorated rooms that exude old-world charm. Guests can enjoy gourmet breakfasts and take advantage of the property's proximity to local attractions and beaches. The serene setting and luxurious amenities make it ideal for romantic getaways. For pricing and reservations, visit their website.

Strawberry House Bed and Breakfast: Located in the heart of Plant City's historic district, Strawberry House offers guests a delightful stay in a beautifully restored Dutch Colonial home. Each of the five suites is uniquely furnished with antiques and collectibles, providing a cozy and nostalgic atmosphere. Guests are treated to a delicious breakfast each morning and can explore the nearby antique shops and local attractions. The bed and breakfast's proximity to the annual Florida Strawberry Festival makes it a popular choice during the event. Room rates and availability can be found on their website. Each of these bed and breakfasts offers a distinctive experience, allowing visitors to Tampa to choose accommodations that best suit their preferences and enhance their stay in this vibrant city.

CHAPTER 3
TRANSPORTATION

3.1 Getting to Tampa

Tampa, a vibrant city on Florida's Gulf Coast, is accessible through various modes of transportation, each offering unique experiences for travelers. Whether you prefer the convenience of air travel, the scenic journey by train, or the flexibility of road trips, reaching Tampa is straightforward and accommodating to different preferences and budgets.

Arriving by Air: For those opting for air travel, Tampa International Airport (TPA) serves as the primary gateway to the city. Recognized for its efficient layout and passenger-friendly services, TPA hosts numerous airlines offering flights from various destinations. Major carriers such as American Airlines, United Airlines, and Delta Air Lines operate regular flights to Tampa. Ticket prices fluctuate based on factors like departure city, booking time, and season. For instance, flights from New York to Tampa can start as low as $90 for a round trip, depending on the airline and booking period. To secure the best fares, it's advisable to book in advance through the airlines' official websites or reputable travel platforms like Expedia or Kayak. Always review the terms and conditions, including baggage allowances and change fees, before finalizing your booking.

Traveling by Train: If a leisurely journey appeals to you, Amtrak provides train services to Tampa, offering a scenic and relaxed travel experience. The Silver Star route connects cities along the East Coast to Tampa, with services from locations such as Jacksonville and Orlando. For example, a train ride from Jacksonville to Tampa takes approximately 5 hours and 29 minutes, with ticket prices starting around $28. Amtrak's trains feature amenities like comfortable seating, dining options, and Wi-Fi, ensuring a pleasant journey. Tickets can be purchased through Amtrak's official website or at station ticket counters. It's recommended to book ahead, especially during peak travel seasons, to secure preferred seating and accommodations.

Reaching Tampa by Road: For travelers who enjoy the freedom of road trips, Tampa is well-connected by an extensive network of highways, making it accessible from various parts of Florida and neighboring states. Interstate 75 runs north-south, while Interstate 4 connects Tampa to Orlando and the eastern regions. Bus services, such as Greyhound and Megabus, offer routes to Tampa from numerous cities. For instance, Greyhound provides services from Miami to Tampa, with fares starting around $12.48. The journey duration varies depending on the departure point; from Miami, it typically takes about 7 hours and 20 minutes. Tickets can be booked online through the bus companies' websites or purchased at bus terminals. For those driving, numerous car rental agencies operate in and around Tampa, providing flexibility to explore the city and its surroundings at your own pace.

Additional Considerations: When planning your trip to Tampa, consider factors such as travel time, budget, and personal preferences. Air travel offers speed and convenience, ideal for long-distance travelers. Train journeys provide a scenic and relaxed experience, suitable for those who appreciate the journey as part of their adventure. Road travel, whether by bus or car, offers flexibility and the opportunity to explore various attractions along the way. Always check the latest travel schedules, ticket prices, and any travel advisories before your departure to ensure a smooth and enjoyable journey to Tampa.

3.2 Public Transportation Options

Tampa, Florida, offers a variety of public transportation options that cater to both residents and visitors, making it convenient to explore the city's attractions without the need for a personal vehicle.

Hillsborough Area Regional Transit Authority (HART): HART operates an extensive bus network throughout Tampa and its surrounding areas, providing an affordable and accessible means of transportation. The standard fare for a one-way trip is $2.00, with discounted rates available for seniors, students, and individuals with disabilities. For frequent travelers, HART offers unlimited ride passes, including a 1-day pass for $4.00 and a 31-day pass for $65.00. Tickets can be purchased directly from bus operators upon boarding or through the Flamingo Fares app, which also provides real-time bus tracking and route information. The main hub, Marion Transit Center, located in downtown Tampa, serves as a central point for many routes, facilitating easy transfers and access to various parts of the city. gohart.org

TECO Line Streetcar System: For a nostalgic journey through some of Tampa's most historic districts, the TECO Line Streetcar offers a charming and convenient option. Connecting Ybor City, the Channel District, and downtown Tampa, this 2.7-mile route features 11 stations with streetcars arriving approximately every 15 minutes. As of October 2018, rides are free for all passengers, thanks to a grant from the Florida Department of Transportation. The streetcars are wheelchair accessible, and each station provides covered waiting areas. Operating hours vary, with extended service during special events and weekends, making it a practical choice for both daytime sightseeing and evening outings. tecolinestreetcar.org

Pirate Water Taxi: Offering a unique perspective of the city, the Pirate Water Taxi navigates the Hillsborough River with 14 stops along the Tampa Riverwalk, Harbor Island, and Davis Islands. This service operates daily, providing both transportation and narrated tours of Tampa's waterfront landmarks. Tickets can be purchased online or at designated docks, with options for single rides or all-day passes, allowing passengers to hop on and off at their leisure. The water taxis are equipped with comfortable seating and offer a scenic way to travel between popular destinations such as the Tampa Convention Center, Armature Works, and Sparkman Wharf. tampa.gov

Bike Share Programs: For those who prefer an active mode of transportation, Tampa's bike share programs provide a flexible and eco-friendly option. With numerous rental stations throughout the city, particularly along the Tampa Riverwalk and downtown areas, visitors can easily rent bicycles for short trips or extended explorations. Rental fees are typically structured based on duration, with options for hourly or daily rates. Many bike share services offer mobile apps for locating available bikes, making payments, and providing route suggestions, enhancing the convenience for users. Cycling in Tampa allows for a leisurely pace to appreciate the city's parks, waterfront views, and vibrant neighborhoods. citypass.com Each of these public transportation options in Tampa offers unique advantages, catering to different preferences and destinations. Whether opting for the comprehensive bus network of HART, the historic charm of the TECO Line Streetcar, the scenic routes of the Pirate Water Taxi, or the flexibility of bike shares, visitors can navigate the city with ease and convenience.

3.3 Car Rentals and Driving Tips

Exploring Tampa by car offers the freedom to experience the city's diverse attractions at your own pace. Whether you're visiting for business or leisure, renting a vehicle can enhance your stay. Here's an in-depth look at car rental options in Tampa, along with essential driving tips to ensure a smooth journey.

Car Rental Companies in Tampa: Tampa boasts a variety of reputable car rental agencies, each offering a range of vehicles to suit different preferences and budgets. Many of these companies are conveniently located at Tampa International Airport (TPA), providing easy access upon arrival.

Enterprise Rent-A-Car: It operates a branch at 5405 Airport Service Rd, Tampa, FL 33607. They offer a diverse fleet, from compact cars to SUVs, catering to various travel needs. Reservations can be made through their website: https://www.enterprise.com/en/home.html.

Avis Car Rental: It provides services at multiple locations in Tampa, including a counter at Tampa International Airport. They offer amenities such as GPS navigation and a variety of vehicle options. Bookings can be made online at https://www.avis.com/en/locations/us/fl/tampa.

Budget Rent a Car: This has several outlets in Tampa, offering a wide selection of vehicles suitable for both short-term and long-term rentals. Their user-friendly website allows for easy reservations: https://www.budget.com/en/locations/us/fl/tampa.

Alamo Rent A Car: erves travelers at Tampa International Airport, with a variety of vehicles to choose from. Their streamlined booking process can be accessed at https://www.alamo.com/en/car-rental-locations/us/fl/tampa-international-airport-42f6.html.

Hertz: Hertz offers car rental services throughout Tampa, providing a range of vehicles from economy cars to luxury models. Reservations can be made via their website: https://www.hertz.com/us/en/location/unitedstates/florida/tampa.

Fox Rent A Car: Located at 5405 Airport Service Road, Suite C-403, Tampa, FL 33607-1419. They offer competitive rates and a variety of vehicle options. For bookings, visit https://www.foxrentacar.com/en/locations/united-states/florida/tampa-airport.html Rental rates in Tampa vary based on factors such as vehicle type, rental duration, and demand. On average, daily rates can range from $30 for economy cars to over $100 for luxury vehicles. It's advisable to book in advance, especially during peak travel seasons, to secure the best rates and vehicle availability.

Driving Tips in Tampa: Navigating Tampa's roads requires awareness of local driving conditions and regulations. The city experiences peak traffic during morning (7:00 AM to 9:00 AM) and evening (4:00 PM to 6:30 PM) rush hours. Planning your travel outside these times can help you avoid congestion. Additionally, be prepared for increased traffic near popular attractions and event venues, especially on weekends. Florida law permits right turns at red lights after a complete stop, unless otherwise indicated by signage. Always be vigilant for pedestrians and oncoming traffic before proceeding. Speed limits are strictly enforced, with typical limits of 30 mph in urban areas and 70 mph on interstate highways. Adhering to these limits is crucial for safety and to avoid fines. Parking in downtown Tampa includes both metered street parking and parking garages. It's important to observe parking regulations to avoid fines or towing. Some areas offer mobile payment options for added convenience. Tampa employs traffic cameras to monitor red light compliance. Even if law enforcement is not present, violations can result in tickets being mailed to the vehicle's registered owner. Therefore, it's essential to obey all traffic signals and signs. Driving in Tampa can be fast-paced, with some drivers exhibiting aggressive behaviors. Maintaining a calm demeanor, avoiding confrontations, and practicing defensive driving are key to navigating the roads safely. Always use turn signals, avoid sudden lane changes, and be courteous to other drivers. By familiarizing yourself with these car rental options and driving tips, you'll be well-prepared to explore Tampa confidently and safely. Enjoy the journey as you discover all that this vibrant city has to offer.

3.4 Walking and Cycling Trails
Tampa, Florida, offers a variety of scenic walking and cycling trails that showcase the city's natural beauty and vibrant communities. These trails provide residents and visitors with opportunities to explore diverse landscapes, from waterfront vistas to lush greenways.

Tampa Riverwalk: The Tampa Riverwalk is a 2.6-mile (4 km) trail that meanders along the Hillsborough River and Garrison Channel, connecting downtown's prominent attractions. Starting near The Florida Aquarium, it passes by landmarks such as the Tampa Bay History Center, Curtis Hixon Waterfront Park, and the Straz Center for the Performing Arts. The wide, paved pathway is ideal for both walkers and cyclists, offering picturesque views of the river and city skyline. Access points are available throughout downtown, with parking options nearby. The Riverwalk is open year-round, providing a scenic route for exercise and leisure. visittampabay.com

Upper Tampa Bay Trail: The Upper Tampa Bay Trail is a 7.25-mile route that winds through northwest Hillsborough County. The trail features a mix of shaded areas and open spaces, with amenities such as restrooms, water fountains, and picnic spots along the way. Trailheads with parking are located at various points, including on Montague Street off Memorial Highway.

Courtney Campbell Trail: The Courtney Campbell Trail is a 9.5-mile paved pathway that parallels the Courtney Campbell Causeway, connecting Tampa to Clearwater. The trail offers expansive views of Tampa Bay, with a notable 45-foot incline over the bridge providing a rewarding challenge for cyclists. Access points are available on both the Tampa and Clearwater sides, with parking facilities at Cypress Point Park in Tampa. The trail is open year-round, offering a scenic route for both casual and experienced riders. westchasewow.com

Bayshore Linear Park Trail: Bayshore Linear Park Trail, also known as the "World's Longest Continuous Sidewalk," stretches 4.5 miles along Bayshore Boulevard. The trail offers panoramic views of Tampa Bay and is adorned with decorative balustrades and historic light fixtures. Access points are available along Bayshore Boulevard, with parking options nearby.

Flatwoods Park Trail: Flatwoods Park Trail is an 8-mile loop located within Flatwoods Park in northeastern Tampa. The paved pathway meanders through pine flatwoods and cypress domes, offering a serene environment for outdoor activities. The park features amenities such as restrooms, water stations, and picnic areas. Access is available via the park's main entrance on Morris Bridge Road, with parking facilities on-site. The trail is open daily from sunrise to sunset, providing a peaceful retreat for nature enthusiasts. Each of these trails offers a unique experience, allowing visitors to immerse themselves in Tampa's diverse landscapes and vibrant communities. Whether seeking a leisurely stroll along the waterfront or an invigorating bike ride through natural preserves, Tampa's trail network provides ample opportunities for exploration and recreation.

3.5 Shuttle Services

Navigating Tampa is made convenient by a variety of shuttle services catering to both residents and visitors. These services offer reliable transportation options across the city and to key destinations.

SuperShuttle Tampa Bay: SuperShuttle Tampa Bay provides transportation to and from Tampa International Airport (TPA), Sarasota-Bradenton International Airport (SRQ), and St. Pete–Clearwater International Airport (PIE). They offer private black car, SUV, and van services, accommodating individual travelers and groups.

Reservations can be made through their website: https://www.supershuttle.com/locations/tampa-tpa/. Pricing varies based on the selected service and distance, with options for shared rides and exclusive vehicles.

Tampa Bay Airport Shuttle Service: With over 15 years of experience, Tampa Bay Airport Shuttle Service offers airport, cruise, and theme park shuttle services. They provide prompt and affordable transportation, ensuring timely arrivals and departures. Prices depend on the destination and number of passengers, with options for both one-way and round-trip services.

Blue One Transportation Services: Blue One Transportation Services specializes in private shuttle services throughout Tampa and its surrounding areas. They offer professional, safe, and reliable transportation, serving as a cost-effective alternative to traditional taxis. Their services can be accessed via their website: https://blueonetransportation.com/. Pricing is competitive and varies based on the specific transportation needs of the client.

Express Transportation: Express Transportation provides shuttle services to and from Tampa International Airport, the Port of Tampa, and various hotels. Known for their affordable, reliable, and fast service, they cater to both individual travelers and groups. Reservations can be made by calling 813-731-9283 or through their website: https://www.expresstransportationnow.com/. Prices are reasonable and depend on the destination and number of passengers.

Alora Transportation: Alora Transportation offers shuttle and black car services to Tampa International Airport and point-to-point transportation around the Tampa Bay area. They provide a variety of ride choices to fit different budgets, from non-stop airport shuttles to private black car services. Bookings can be made online at https://aloraride.com/ or by calling 866-276-0882. Pricing varies based on the selected service and distance.

Hillsborough Area Regional Transit (HART): HART provides public transportation services throughout Hillsborough County, including bus and streetcar services. While not a private shuttle service, HART offers an affordable and reliable means of transportation within Tampa. Information on routes, schedules, and fares can be found on their website: http://www.gohart.org/. Fares are economical, with various pass options available to suit different travel needs. When selecting a shuttle service in Tampa, consider factors such as destination, budget, and preferred level of privacy. Booking in advance is recommended, especially during peak travel times, to ensure availability and secure the best rates.

CHAPTER 4
TOP 10 ATTRACTIONS & HIDDEN GEMS

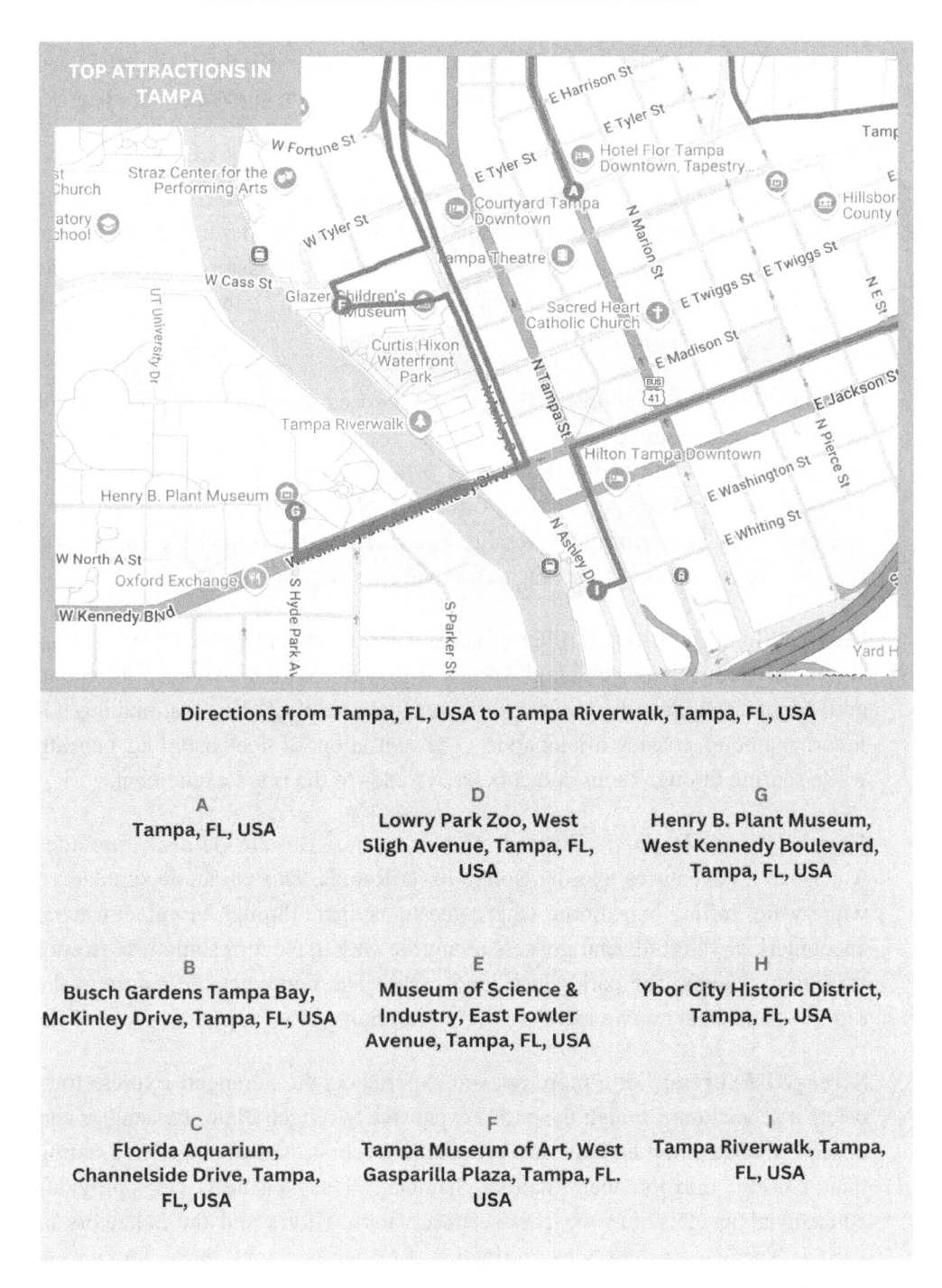

Directions from Tampa, FL, USA to Tampa Riverwalk, Tampa, FL, USA

A
Tampa, FL, USA

B
Busch Gardens Tampa Bay, McKinley Drive, Tampa, FL, USA

C
Florida Aquarium, Channelside Drive, Tampa, FL, USA

D
Lowry Park Zoo, West Sligh Avenue, Tampa, FL, USA

E
Museum of Science & Industry, East Fowler Avenue, Tampa, FL, USA

F
Tampa Museum of Art, West Gasparilla Plaza, Tampa, FL. USA

G
Henry B. Plant Museum, West Kennedy Boulevard, Tampa, FL, USA

H
Ybor City Historic District, Tampa, FL, USA

I
Tampa Riverwalk, Tampa, FL, USA

36

4.1 Busch Gardens Tampa Bay

Busch Gardens Tampa Bay stands as a premier destination for thrill-seekers and families alike, seamlessly blending exhilarating rides with immersive animal exhibits. Located at 10165 McKinley Drive in Tampa, Florida, this renowned theme park offers a diverse array of attractions that captivate visitors of all ages.

SheiKra: Among the park's most iconic roller coasters is SheiKra, a dive coaster that ascends to a height of 200 feet before plunging riders at a 90-degree angle into a subterranean tunnel. This heart-pounding experience provides an unparalleled adrenaline rush, making it a must-ride for coaster enthusiasts. The sheer vertical drop and subsequent inversions offer a unique thrill that sets SheiKra apart from other attractions.

Cheetah Hunt: For those seeking a high-speed adventure, Cheetah Hunt delivers with its triple-launch system that propels riders through a sprawling track inspired by the swift movements of a cheetah. Spanning 4,400 feet, it stands as the park's longest coaster, offering a blend of speed, twists, and turns that mimic the agility of its namesake. The ride's design provides a smooth yet exhilarating experience, appealing to a broad spectrum of visitors.

Montu: Montu, an inverted roller coaster, offers a different kind of thrill with its seven intense inversions and high-speed drops. Named after an ancient Egyptian god, Montu combines theming with adrenaline-pumping elements, making it a favorite among coaster aficionados. The sensation of feet dangling beneath while soaring through loops and corkscrews adds to the ride's excitement.

Congo River Rapids: Beyond the coasters, Busch Gardens provides water-based adventures like the Congo River Rapids. This attraction simulates a white-water rafting expedition, where guests navigate through turbulent waters, encountering waterfalls and geysers along the way. It's a refreshing way to cool off while enjoying the park's lush landscapes. The unpredictable nature of the rapids ensures that no two rides are the same, adding to its appeal.

Serengeti Express: For a more relaxed experience, the Serengeti Express train offers a scenic tour through the park's expansive Serengeti Plain. Passengers can observe free-roaming animals such as giraffes, zebras, and antelopes in a setting that closely mirrors their natural habitats. This leisurely ride provides educational insights into the park's conservation efforts and the behaviors of various species. It's an ideal attraction for families and those looking to appreciate the park's commitment to wildlife preservation. Admission to Busch Gardens Tampa Bay varies, with options for single-day tickets, multi-day passes, and annual memberships. Purchasing tickets online in advance often provides discounts and ensures availability, especially during peak seasons. The park operates year-round, with hours that may vary depending on the time of year and special events. Visitors are encouraged to check the official website for the most up-to-date information on operating hours, ticket prices, and health and safety guidelines. Busch Gardens Tampa Bay offers a harmonious blend of thrilling rides and immersive animal encounters, making it a must-visit destination for those seeking both adventure and education. Its diverse attractions cater to a wide range of interests, ensuring a memorable experience for all who enter its gates.

4.2 Florida Aquarium

Tampa, Florida, is a city filled with breathtaking sights, fascinating history, and world-class attractions. Whether you love marine life, lush gardens, or cultural landmarks, Tampa offers a perfect mix of adventure and relaxation. From immersive aquariums to scenic parks, each location promises an unforgettable experience for visitors of all ages.

The Florida Aquarium: Located in downtown Tampa, The Florida Aquarium is one of the city's top destinations for marine life enthusiasts. It houses thousands of aquatic species, including sharks, stingrays, sea turtles, and playful otters.

Visitors can explore interactive exhibits, a massive coral reef, and even a wetlands trail showcasing native Florida wildlife. The aquarium also offers a unique Wild Dolphin Cruise, where guests can spot dolphins in Tampa Bay. General admission prices start at $32.95 for adults, with discounts for children and seniors.

Busch Gardens Tampa Bay: Busch Gardens is a thrilling combination of a zoo and theme park, offering adrenaline-pumping rides and up-close animal encounters. Located about 10 miles from downtown Tampa, it features world-class roller coasters, including Iron Gwazi and SheiKra. Visitors can explore the Serengeti Safari, home to giraffes, zebras, and rhinos, or enjoy live shows and seasonal events. The park celebrates African culture with themed villages, exotic cuisine, and immersive experiences. General admission starts at $99.99, with annual passes and combo tickets available.

Tampa Riverwalk: Stretching along the Hillsborough River, the Tampa Riverwalk is a scenic pathway connecting the city's best attractions. It's the perfect spot for a leisurely stroll, bike ride, or even a sunset cruise along the water. Along the way, visitors can explore museums, parks, restaurants, and public art displays. The Riverwalk hosts frequent events, including food festivals and live music performances. Best of all, it's free to visit, making it an ideal destination for budget-conscious travelers.

Ybor City: Ybor City is Tampa's historic district, known for its rich Cuban heritage, vibrant nightlife, and famous hand-rolled cigars. Founded in the 1880s by Vicente Martinez-Ybor, this neighborhood was once the cigar capital of the world. Today, visitors can explore its charming brick streets, dine at authentic Cuban restaurants, and visit the Ybor City Museum State Park. The area comes alive at night with lively bars, flamenco dancing, and Latin music. Walking tours are available to learn about its history, with most attractions free to explore.

ZooTampa at Lowry Park: ZooTampa is a must-visit for animal lovers, offering interactive experiences with rare and endangered species. Home to more than 1,300 animals, the zoo features a manatee rehabilitation center, a primate reserve, and a large African habitat. Visitors can enjoy up-close encounters with koalas, rhinos, and even feed giraffes. The zoo focuses on conservation and education, making it both fun and informative for families.

General admission starts at $44.95 for adults, with discounts available for children and Florida residents. Each of these attractions captures the essence of Tampa, blending adventure, history, and wildlife. Whether exploring marine life, thrilling roller coasters, or cultural heritage, visitors are guaranteed an unforgettable experience.

4.3 Lowry Park Zoo

ZooTampa at Lowry Park stands as a premier destination in Tampa, Florida, offering visitors an immersive experience with wildlife from around the globe. Located at 1101 West Sligh Avenue, the zoo is easily accessible by car via I-275, with ample on-site parking available. Public transportation options, such as the HART bus system, also provide convenient routes to the zoo. Admission prices vary, with discounts available for children, seniors, and military personnel. Purchasing tickets online in advance is recommended to expedite entry. The zoo operates daily, with hours that may vary seasonally, so it's advisable to check their official website for the most current information.

Manatee Critical Care Center: One of the zoo's most significant features is the David A. Straz, Jr. Manatee Critical Care Center. This facility is dedicated to the rescue, rehabilitation, and release of injured or ill manatees, offering guests a unique opportunity to observe these gentle giants up close. Educational displays provide insights into the challenges manatees face in the wild and the conservation efforts underway to protect them. Witnessing the compassionate care provided to these endangered creatures underscores the zoo's commitment to wildlife preservation.

Safari Africa: Embarking on a journey through Safari Africa transports visitors to the savannas of the African continent. This expansive exhibit is home to majestic species such as African elephants, giraffes, and white rhinoceroses. The immersive design allows guests to observe these animals in settings that closely resemble their natural habitats. Interactive experiences, like feeding giraffes, offer memorable encounters that foster a deeper appreciation for these magnificent creatures.

Primate World: Primate World showcases a diverse array of primate species, including Bornean orangutans, siamang gibbons, and mandrills. The thoughtfully designed habitats feature lush vegetation and intricate climbing structures, encouraging natural behaviors and providing an engaging environment for both the animals and visitors. Observing the complex social interactions and playful antics of these intelligent creatures offers a captivating glimpse into the world of primates.

Wallaroo Station: For families with young children, Wallaroo Station presents an Australian-themed children's zoo complete with interactive exhibits and engaging activities. This area features a variety of attractions, including a splash pad, petting zoo, and gentle rides suitable for younger guests. Encounters with koalas, kangaroos, and other Australian wildlife provide educational opportunities in a fun and accessible setting. The vibrant atmosphere and hands-on experiences make it a favorite destination for families visiting the zoo.

Florida Boardwalk: The Florida Boardwalk offers a journey through the diverse ecosystems of the Sunshine State. Shaded pathways guide visitors past exhibits housing native species such as alligators, black bears, and the elusive Florida panther. Educational signage highlights the importance of these animals to Florida's natural heritage and the conservation efforts aimed at ensuring their survival. The boardwalk setting, complete with lush vegetation and the sounds of native wildlife, immerses guests in the unique environments found throughout the state. A visit to ZooTampa at Lowry Park provides a comprehensive and enriching experience, blending entertainment with education and conservation. The thoughtfully curated exhibits and interactive opportunities inspire a deeper understanding and appreciation for wildlife, making it a must-see attraction for anyone visiting the Tampa area.

4.4 Museum of Science and Industry

Tampa, Florida, is a city brimming with diverse attractions that cater to a wide range of interests. From interactive science exhibits to thrilling amusement parks, Tampa offers experiences that captivate visitors of all ages.

Museum of Science and Industry (MOSI): Located at 4801 E Fowler Avenue, MOSI is a hands-on science center dedicated to making science, technology, engineering, arts, and math (STEAM) accessible to all. Visitors can explore over 100 interactive exhibits, including the Dinovations Lab, where paleontology comes to life, and the Connectus exhibit, showcasing cutting-edge technology. The Saunders Planetarium offers a journey through the cosmos, providing a stellar experience for astronomy enthusiasts. General admission is $14 for adults and $10 for children aged 3-17, with additional fees for special exhibits and experiences. MOSI's commitment to interactive learning makes it a must-visit destination for families and science aficionados.

Busch Gardens Tampa Bay: Situated at 10165 N McKinley Drive, Busch Gardens combines the thrill of an amusement park with the allure of a zoo. Spanning 335 acres, it features adrenaline-pumping roller coasters like SheiKra and Tigris, as well as live entertainment and up-close animal encounters. The Serengeti Plain offers a safari experience, allowing visitors to observe giraffes, zebras, and other African wildlife in a naturalistic setting. Admission prices vary, with options for single-day tickets and annual passes. The park's blend of excitement and education makes it a top attraction in Tampa.

The Florida Aquarium: Located in the Channelside District at 701 Channelside Drive, The Florida Aquarium is home to over 7,000 aquatic plants and animals. Exhibits like "Journey to Madagascar" and "Bays & Beaches" offer insights into diverse ecosystems. Interactive experiences, such as the Stingray Touch Tank and the 4-D Theater, engage visitors in marine conservation efforts. General admission is approximately $33, with discounts available for children and seniors. The aquarium's dedication to education and conservation provides a captivating experience for all ages.

Tampa Riverwalk: Extending 2.6 miles along the Hillsborough River, the Tampa Riverwalk connects several of the city's attractions, parks, and eateries.

This scenic pathway offers picturesque views of the downtown skyline and is adorned with public art installations. Visitors can rent bikes or take leisurely strolls, stopping at points of interest like the Tampa Museum of Art and the Glazer Children's Museum. The Riverwalk is free to access and often hosts community events, making it a vibrant hub of activity.

Ybor City: Founded in the 1880s by cigar manufacturers, Ybor City is a historic neighborhood known for its rich cultural heritage. Located northeast of downtown Tampa, it boasts a blend of Cuban, Spanish, and Italian influences. The brick-lined streets are home to eclectic shops, authentic restaurants, and vibrant nightlife. The Ybor City Museum State Park offers insights into the area's history, while the annual Ybor City Cigar Festival celebrates its legacy. Visiting Ybor City provides a unique glimpse into Tampa's multicultural past and present. Each of these attractions offers a distinct experience, showcasing the diverse offerings that make Tampa a compelling destination for travelers.

4.5 Tampa Museum of Art

The Tampa Museum of Art, located along the scenic Hillsborough River in downtown Tampa, stands as a beacon of cultural enrichment and artistic exploration. Its sleek, modern architecture houses a diverse array of exhibitions that captivate and inspire visitors. Easily accessible via major roadways and public transportation, the museum offers ample parking and is within walking distance of other downtown attractions. Admission fees are structured to accommodate various audiences, with discounts available for students, seniors, and military personnel. Notably, the museum hosts "Art on the House" every Thursday from 4 to 8 pm, allowing guests to pay what they wish for admission, making art accessible to all.

Esterio Segura: One of the museum's standout installations is "Hybrid of a Chrysler" by Cuban artist Esterio Segura. This thought-provoking piece features a 1953 Chrysler Windsor adorned with wings, symbolizing themes of freedom, isolation, and desire. The artwork invites viewers to reflect on the complexities of Cuban life and the universal quest for liberation. Its striking visual presence and profound symbolism make it a must-see for art enthusiasts.

Joseph Veach Noble Collection: The museum's permanent collection boasts an impressive array of ancient artifacts, with a significant focus on Greek and Roman antiquities. Acquired in 1986, the Joseph Veach Noble Collection includes over 175 objects, offering insights into ancient civilizations through pottery, sculpture, and everyday items. This collection provides a tangible connection to the past, enriching visitors' understanding of historical cultures.

Vaughn Spann: Contemporary art enthusiasts will appreciate the works of Vaughn Spann, whose exhibition "Allegories" merges abstraction and figuration. His vibrant paintings, characterized by bold colors and dynamic compositions, explore themes of identity, experience, and the human condition. Spann's art challenges viewers to engage with complex narratives, making for a compelling and introspective experience.

Under the Spell of the Palm Tree The Rice Collection of Cuban Art: This exhibition showcases a diverse selection of modern and contemporary Cuban artworks, encompassing paintings, drawings, photographs, and sculptures. Organized thematically, it delves into various aspects of Cuban culture, history, and identity. The collection offers a comprehensive overview of the island's rich artistic heritage, providing context and depth to the nation's creative expressions.

The Etruscans: For those fascinated by ancient civilizations, the upcoming exhibition on the Etruscans presents a rare glimpse into this enigmatic culture. Featuring artifacts that highlight the art and daily life of the Etruscan people, the display aims to shed light on their contributions to history and their enduring mysteries. It's an educational journey that enriches one's appreciation for ancient societies.Visiting the Tampa Museum of Art offers a multifaceted experience that bridges the ancient and modern worlds. Its thoughtfully curated exhibitions and engaging programs make it a cornerstone of Tampa's cultural landscape, inviting all to explore and be inspired.

4.6 Henry B. Plant Museum

Visitors can explore exhibits that highlight the hotel's role during the Spanish-American War and its significance in Tampa's development. Admission is $10 for adults and $7 for seniors and students. Visitors can easily drive to the museum, with ample parking available on the premises. A visit here immerses guests in a bygone era of elegance and innovation.

Tampa Museum of Art: Situated at 120 West Gasparilla Plaza, the Tampa Museum of Art boasts a diverse collection ranging from ancient to contemporary works. The museum's modern architecture provides a striking contrast to its historical exhibits, creating a dynamic space for art appreciation. Special exhibitions and educational programs offer insights into various artistic movements and cultural narratives. General admission is $15, with discounts for students, seniors, and military personnel. The museum's location along the Tampa Riverwalk makes it a convenient stop for those exploring downtown. Art enthusiasts will find the museum's offerings both enriching and inspiring.

Ybor City: Once known as the "Cigar Capital of the World," Ybor City is a historic neighborhood that reflects Tampa's multicultural heritage. Founded in the 1880s by cigar manufacturers, it became a melting pot of Cuban, Spanish, and Italian immigrants. Today, visitors can stroll along its brick-lined streets, visit authentic cigar shops, and dine in establishments that serve traditional cuisines. The Ybor City Museum State Park provides deeper insights into the area's history and cultural significance. Accessible via the TECO Line Streetcar, Ybor City offers a vibrant atmosphere that captures the essence of Tampa's diverse roots.

Busch Gardens Tampa Bay: For those seeking adventure, Busch Gardens Tampa Bay at 10165 North McKinley Drive combines thrilling rides with wildlife encounters. This African-themed amusement park features roller coasters, live entertainment, and a vast array of animal exhibits. Guests can embark on safari tours to observe giraffes, zebras, and other exotic species up close. Admission prices vary, with options for single-day tickets and annual passes. The park's blend of excitement and education makes it a must-visit destination for families and thrill-seekers alike.

Tampa Riverwalk: Connecting several of the city's attractions, the Tampa Riverwalk is a scenic 2.6-mile pathway along the Hillsborough River. It links parks, museums, and entertainment venues, providing a picturesque route for walking, biking, or leisurely exploration. Along the way, visitors can enjoy public art installations, waterfront views, and access to dining options. The Riverwalk also hosts various events throughout the year, enhancing its appeal as a central gathering place. It's an ideal way to experience the city's vibrant atmosphere and natural beauty. Each of these attractions offers a unique window into Tampa's rich tapestry of history, culture, and entertainment. Whether you're delving into the opulence of the Henry B. Plant Museum or enjoying the lively ambiance of Ybor City, Tampa provides a diverse array of experiences that cater to all interests.

4.7 Ybor City Historic District

Ybor City Historic District in Tampa, Florida, is a vibrant enclave teeming with rich history, diverse culture, and a lively atmosphere. Established in the late 19th century by cigar manufacturers, it has evolved into a must-visit destination for those seeking to immerse themselves in Tampa's unique heritage.

Ybor City Museum State Park: At the heart of the district lies the Ybor City Museum State Park, housed in the historic Ferlita Bakery building at 1818 East 9th Avenue. This museum offers a comprehensive look into the area's past, focusing on the cigar industry's pivotal role in shaping the community. Visitors can explore exhibits that showcase the lives of the immigrants who built Ybor City, providing a window into their daily experiences. The adjacent Mediterranean-style garden offers a tranquil space to reflect on the rich narratives presented within. An admission fee of $4 grants access to both the museum and the serene garden.

Columbia Restaurant: A culinary landmark, the Columbia Restaurant at 2117 East 7th Avenue has been serving patrons since 1905. As Florida's oldest restaurant, it offers an authentic Spanish-Cuban dining experience, with signature dishes like the "1905 Salad" and traditional paella. The establishment's ornate décor, featuring hand-painted tiles and elegant fountains, transports guests to a bygone era. Dining here is not just about the food; it's an immersion into the cultural tapestry that defines Ybor City.

Centro Ybor: Situated at 1600 East 8th Avenue, Centro Ybor is a dynamic entertainment complex that seamlessly blends the historic charm of Ybor City with modern attractions. Visitors can enjoy a variety of experiences, from catching a movie at the theater to exploring unique boutiques and savoring diverse culinary offerings. The complex serves as a central hub, reflecting the district's evolution while honoring its storied past.

7th Avenue: Often referred to as "La Septima," 7th Avenue is the main thoroughfare of Ybor City, renowned for its vibrant energy and historic significance. Lined with an eclectic mix of shops, restaurants, and nightlife venues, the street offers a sensory feast for visitors. The well-preserved architecture provides a glimpse into the district's rich history, making a stroll down 7th Avenue both a cultural and visual delight.

The Cuban Club: Located at 2010 North Avenida Republica de Cuba, the Cuban Club, or "El Circulo Cubano," is a historic landmark that once served as a social hub for Cuban immigrants. Today, it stands as a testament to the community's enduring spirit, hosting a variety of events and performances. The building's architectural grandeur and cultural significance make it a must-see attraction for those interested in the rich tapestry of Ybor City's heritage. Visiting Ybor City Historic District offers a journey through time, where each attraction provides a unique lens into the area's multifaceted history and culture. Whether you're savoring traditional cuisine, exploring historical exhibits, or simply soaking in the vibrant street life, Ybor City promises an enriching and unforgettable experience.

4.8 Tampa Riverwalk

The Tampa Riverwalk is a 2.6-mile pedestrian pathway that gracefully traces the contours of the Hillsborough River, weaving through the heart of downtown Tampa. This scenic corridor not only offers picturesque waterfront views but also connects visitors to a myriad of cultural, historical, and recreational attractions. Exploring the Riverwalk provides an immersive experience into the vibrant tapestry of Tampa's urban landscape.

Curtis Hixon Waterfront Park: Located along the Riverwalk at 600 North Ashley Drive, Curtis Hixon Waterfront Park serves as a central gathering space for both locals and tourists. Spanning over eight acres, the park features open lawns, interactive fountains, and a modern playground. Its design seamlessly integrates with the river, offering unobstructed views of the water and city skyline. The park frequently hosts concerts, festivals, and community events, making it a lively hub of activity year-round. Admission is free, and its central location makes it easily accessible by foot, bike, or public transportation. Visiting Curtis Hixon Waterfront Park provides a refreshing urban oasis where one can relax, play, or partake in Tampa's vibrant community events.

Tampa Museum of Art: Adjacent to Curtis Hixon Park at 120 West Gasparilla Plaza, the Tampa Museum of Art stands as a beacon of modern design and artistic expression. The museum's collection encompasses a diverse range of works, from ancient Greek and Roman antiquities to contemporary art installations. Special exhibitions rotate throughout the year, ensuring a fresh experience with each visit. The museum also offers educational programs, workshops, and lectures aimed at fostering an appreciation for the visual arts. General admission is $15 for adults, with discounted rates for seniors, students, and military personnel. Exploring the Tampa Museum of Art provides a cultural enrichment that complements the natural beauty of the Riverwalk.

Glazer Children's Museum: Located at 110 West Gasparilla Plaza, adjacent to the Tampa Museum of Art, the Glazer Children's Museum is a haven for young minds eager to explore and learn. Designed for children up to 10 years old, the museum offers interactive exhibits that encourage imaginative play and hands-on discovery. From a kid-sized grocery store to a water play zone, each exhibit is crafted to educate and entertain simultaneously. The museum also hosts camps, workshops, and special events tailored to various age groups. Admission is $15 for children and adults, with discounts available for seniors and military families. A visit to the Glazer Children's Museum provides a delightful and educational experience for families traversing the Riverwalk.

Tampa Bay History Center: Situated further along the Riverwalk at 801 Water Street, the Tampa Bay History Center delves into the rich and diverse history of the Tampa Bay region. The museum's exhibits span 12,000 years, covering indigenous cultures, Spanish exploration, and the evolution of modern Tampa. Interactive displays, artifacts, and multimedia presentations bring the past to life, offering insights into the area's cultural and historical development. The center also features the Columbia Cafe, where visitors can savor traditional Cuban cuisine in a setting that echoes Tampa's historic Ybor City. Admission is $14.95 for adults, with reduced rates for seniors, students, and children. Exploring the Tampa Bay History Center provides a comprehensive understanding of the forces that have shaped this vibrant city.

Armature Works: At the northern terminus of the Riverwalk, located at 1910 North Ola Avenue, lies Armature Works, a revitalized mixed-use space that has become a culinary and cultural hotspot. Housed in a historic streetcar warehouse, Armature Works features the Heights Public Market, an eclectic food hall offering a diverse array of dining options. Beyond its culinary offerings, the venue hosts artisan markets, live music, and community events, fostering a dynamic atmosphere that appeals to a broad audience. The expansive outdoor lawn provides a perfect setting for picnics, games, or simply soaking in the riverside ambiance. There is no entry fee to Armature Works, though individual vendors set their own prices. Visiting Armature Works offers a contemporary complement to the historical and cultural attractions along the Riverwalk, encapsulating the modern vibrancy of Tampa's urban revival. Traversing the Tampa Riverwalk unveils a curated collection of the city's premier attractions, each offering a unique window into the art, history, and culture that define this dynamic urban landscape. Whether you're seeking educational enrichment, recreational activities, or culinary delights, the Riverwalk serves as a scenic conduit to Tampa's most compelling destinations.

4.9 Fort De Soto Park
Fort De Soto Park, located at 3500 Pinellas Bayway S., Tierra Verde, Florida, is a sprawling 1,136-acre county park renowned for its pristine beaches, rich history, and diverse recreational opportunities. Accessible via the Pinellas Bayway, the park offers ample parking and charges a nominal entrance fee, making it a must-visit destination for both locals and tourists seeking a blend of natural beauty and cultural heritage.

Historic Fort De Soto: At the heart of the park lies the historic fort itself, constructed in the late 19th century as a coastal defense during the Spanish-American War. Visitors can explore the well-preserved fortifications, complete with authentic artillery and informative displays detailing the site's military significance. Walking through the corridors and climbing atop the fort's walls provides a tangible connection to the past, offering panoramic views of the surrounding waterways. This immersive experience makes the fort a highlight for history enthusiasts and casual visitors alike.

North Beach: Renowned for its powdery white sands and clear turquoise waters, North Beach has been consistently ranked among America's top beaches. The expansive shoreline is ideal for sunbathing, swimming, and shelling, while the gentle Gulf waves make it family-friendly. Natural tidal pools often form along the beach, creating perfect spots for children to explore marine life. The unspoiled beauty and serene atmosphere make North Beach a quintessential destination for beach lovers.

Kayak Trails: For adventure seekers, the park offers well-marked kayak trails that meander through lush mangroves and tranquil bayous. Paddlers can rent kayaks on-site and embark on a journey to observe native wildlife, including herons, manatees, and dolphins in their natural habitats. The calm waters and scenic surroundings provide a peaceful escape, allowing visitors to connect deeply with nature. This activity is suitable for both novice and experienced kayakers, offering a unique perspective of the park's ecosystems.

Camping Facilities: Fort De Soto boasts a well-equipped campground with sites that cater to both tent and RV campers. Many sites are waterfront, offering stunning sunrise or sunset views over the bay. Amenities include modern restrooms, laundry facilities, and a camp store for essentials. The serene environment, coupled with the opportunity to observe nocturnal wildlife and stargaze, makes camping here a memorable experience. Reservations are recommended, especially during peak seasons, to secure a spot in this sought-after campground.

Dog Park and Beach: Pet owners will appreciate the dedicated dog park and beach areas where canine companions can roam freely. The fenced dog park provides ample space for dogs to play, while the adjacent dog-friendly beach allows pets to splash in the Gulf waters. Amenities such as dog showers and water stations ensure a comfortable visit for furry friends. This inclusive feature makes Fort De Soto a standout destination for those traveling with pets. Fort De Soto Park offers a harmonious blend of historical intrigue, natural splendor, and recreational activities. Its diverse attractions cater to a wide range of interests, ensuring that every visitor leaves with cherished memories of this coastal gem.

4.10 Clearwater Beach

Clearwater Beach, located on Florida's Gulf Coast, is renowned for its pristine white sands and vibrant coastal attractions. This picturesque destination offers visitors a blend of natural beauty and engaging activities, making it a must-visit spot for those exploring the Tampa Bay area.

Clearwater Beach: Stretching along the Gulf of Mexico, Clearwater Beach boasts soft, sugar-white sands and clear, tranquil waters. The beach is ideal for sunbathing, swimming, and water sports such as parasailing and jet skiing. Its gentle waves make it family-friendly, and the nearby Beach Walk promenade offers a variety of shops and restaurants. Accessible via the Clearwater Memorial Causeway, parking is available in multiple lots, though it can fill up quickly during peak times. Visiting Clearwater Beach provides a quintessential Florida beach experience with modern amenities.

Pier 60: Situated at the heart of Clearwater Beach, Pier 60 is a bustling hub known for its daily sunset celebrations. Each evening, local artisans, street performers, and musicians gather to create a festive atmosphere as the sun dips below the horizon. The pier itself extends into the Gulf, offering fishing opportunities and panoramic views of the coastline. There's no fee to access the main areas, though a small charge applies for those wishing to fish. Pier 60's lively environment and stunning sunsets make it a highlight of any Clearwater visit.

Clearwater Marine Aquarium: Located at 249 Windward Passage, the Clearwater Marine Aquarium is dedicated to the rescue and rehabilitation of marine animals. Home to Winter the dolphin, star of the "Dolphin Tale" films, the facility offers visitors a chance to learn about marine conservation efforts. Interactive exhibits and observation areas allow guests to see dolphins, sea turtles, and otters up close. Admission fees support the aquarium's mission, with tickets priced around $30 for adults and $25 for children. A visit here provides both education and inspiration, highlighting the importance of marine life preservation.

Sand Key Park: Just south of Clearwater Beach, across the Clearwater Pass, lies Sand Key Park at 1060 Gulf Boulevard. This 95-acre park offers a quieter alternative to the bustling main beach. Amenities include picnic shelters, a playground, and a dog-friendly area. The park's beach is expansive, providing ample space for relaxation and shelling. A nominal parking fee applies, but entry to the park is free. Sand Key Park's serene environment makes it a perfect spot for those seeking a peaceful coastal retreat.

Caladesi Island State Park: Accessible by ferry from nearby Honeymoon Island, Caladesi Island State Park offers an untouched natural setting. The island features unspoiled beaches, nature trails, and opportunities for kayaking through mangrove forests. An entry fee of around $6 per boat applies, and the ferry ride is an additional cost. Caladesi's pristine environment provides a glimpse into Florida's coastal ecosystems, making it a must-see for nature enthusiasts. Each of these attractions showcases the unique charm of Clearwater Beach, blending natural beauty with engaging activities. Whether you're seeking relaxation or adventure, Clearwater Beach offers a diverse array of experiences that capture the essence of Florida's Gulf Coast.

4.11 Outdoor Activities and Adventures
Tampa, Florida, offers a plethora of outdoor adventures that cater to nature enthusiasts and thrill-seekers alike. From serene parks to exhilarating zip lines, the city provides diverse experiences that showcase its natural beauty and vibrant culture.

Hillsborough River State Park: Located just minutes from downtown Tampa, Hillsborough River State Park is a sanctuary of natural beauty and historical significance. Visitors can traverse over seven miles of nature trails, winding through lush landscapes and offering glimpses of native wildlife. The park's Class II rapids provide a rare opportunity for kayaking and canoeing enthusiasts to navigate Florida's swift-moving waters. Camping facilities are available for those wishing to immerse themselves in the tranquil ambiance of the Floridian wilderness.

Bayshore Boulevard; Bayshore Boulevard presents a picturesque setting for outdoor enthusiasts, featuring the world's longest continuous sidewalk stretching 4.5 miles along Tampa Bay. Joggers, cyclists, and walkers are treated to panoramic views of the bay's sparkling waters on one side and stately historic homes on the other. The scenic pathway is adorned with decorative balustrades and lighting, enhancing its charm, especially during sunrise and sunset. The boulevard also serves as a venue for community events, fostering a sense of connection among residents and visitors.

Empower Adventures Tampa Bay; For those seeking an adrenaline rush, Empower Adventures Tampa Bay offers a thrilling zip line experience over Mobbly Bayou Wilderness Preserve. Participants can soar up to 65 feet above the ground, enjoying aerial views of the lush landscape below. The guided tours include a series of zip lines, suspension bridges, and a rappel, providing both excitement and a unique perspective of Tampa's natural beauty. Safety is paramount, with experienced guides ensuring a secure and memorable adventure.

Tampa Riverwalk: The Tampa Riverwalk is a vibrant 2.6-mile pedestrian pathway that meanders along the Hillsborough River, connecting numerous parks, museums, and attractions. Visitors can enjoy leisurely strolls, bike rides, or even rent kayaks to explore the river from a different vantage point. The Riverwalk also hosts various festivals and events throughout the year, making it a dynamic hub of activity. Its proximity to dining and entertainment venues enhances the overall experience, offering a seamless blend of urban and natural environments.

Lettuce Lake Park: Situated along the Hillsborough River, Lettuce Lake Park encompasses 240 acres of diverse ecosystems, including hardwood forests, wetlands, and a freshwater lake. A 3,500-foot boardwalk allows visitors to observe wildlife such as herons, alligators, and turtles in their natural habitats. An observation tower provides panoramic views of the surrounding area, while canoe and kayak rentals offer opportunities to explore the serene waterways. The park's picnic areas and playgrounds make it a family-friendly destination, perfect for a day of relaxation and exploration. Engaging in these outdoor activities allows visitors to experience the multifaceted beauty of Tampa, from its tranquil natural parks to its lively urban trails. Each adventure offers a unique perspective, inviting exploration and appreciation of the city's rich landscapes and vibrant community.

4.12 Guided Tours and Recommended Tour Operators

Exploring Tampa's rich history, vibrant culture, and scenic landscapes is best experienced through guided tours that offer insightful narratives and unique perspectives. Several reputable tour operators in Tampa provide diverse experiences to cater to various interests.

Historic Ybor City Food Walking Tour: This tour immerses participants in the flavors and history of Ybor City, Tampa's historic Latin Quarter. Over approximately three hours, guests visit multiple eateries to sample Cuban and Spanish delicacies while learning about the area's cultural heritage. The tour includes generous food and drink tastings, providing a comprehensive culinary experience. More information and bookings are available at https://www.viator.com/Tampa/d666-ttd .

Ybor City Major Walking Tour: This guided tour offers an intimate exploration of Tampa's iconic neighborhoods, including historic Ybor City and the scenic Riverwalk. Conducted in a street-legal golf cart, the tour provides a comfortable and engaging way to see the city's highlights. The knowledgeable guides share insights into Tampa's history, culture, and architecture. Details and reservations can be found on https://www.viator.com/Tampa/d666-ttd .

Tampa History Cruise: For those interested in Tampa's maritime heritage, the Tampa History Cruise offers a unique perspective from the water. This boat tour navigates the Hillsborough River, highlighting significant historical sites and sharing stories of the city's past. It's an informative and relaxing way to appreciate Tampa's waterfront landmarks.

Ybor City Historic Walking Tour: Delving deeper into the rich history of Ybor City, this walking tour explores the district's origins, architecture, and cultural significance. Led by knowledgeable guides, participants visit key landmarks and learn about the influential figures who shaped the area. The tour provides a thorough understanding of this unique neighborhood. Bookings can be made via https://www.viator.com/Tampa/d666-ttd m.

Tampa Bay Fun Boat: Offering a blend of sightseeing and entertainment, Tampa Bay Fun Boat provides tours that showcase the beauty of Tampa's waterways. Guests can enjoy panoramic views of the skyline, spot local wildlife, and learn about the city's history. The relaxed atmosphere makes it suitable for families and groups. More details are available on https://www.tripadvisor.com/Attractions-g34678-Activities-c42-Tampa_Florida.html. Each of these tour operators offers a unique lens through which to experience Tampa, ensuring that visitors can find a tour that aligns with their interests and provides a memorable exploration of the city.

CHAPTER 5
PRACTICAL INFORMATION AND GUIDANCE

5.1 Maps and Navigation

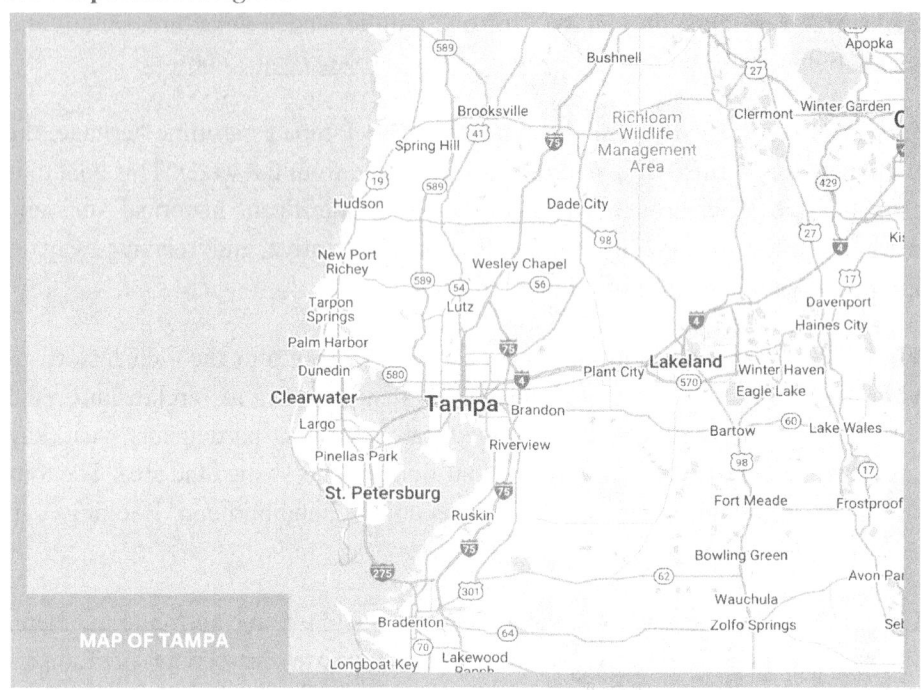

MAP OF TAMPA

SCAN THE QR CODE TO GET A MORE LARGER AND COMPREHENSIVE MAP OF TAMPA

Navigating Tampa is an exciting journey that allows travelers to experience the city's diverse neighborhoods, stunning waterfronts, and vibrant cultural hubs. Whether arriving as a first-time visitor or a seasoned traveler, having reliable maps at your disposal ensures a seamless and immersive experience. From classic paper maps to high-tech digital navigation tools, Tampa offers a variety of resources to help you find your way.

Tampa Tourist Maps and Paper Maps: Traditional paper maps remain a valuable tool for visitors who prefer an offline, tangible guide to the city. Tampa's official tourist maps can be found at major visitor centers, including the Tampa Bay Visitors Information Center in downtown Tampa. Hotels, airports, and attractions such as Busch Gardens and the Tampa Riverwalk also provide printed maps to guests upon request. These maps highlight key points of interest, historic districts, and public transportation routes, making it easier to plan day-to-day itineraries.

Where to Access Offline Paper Maps: Paper maps of Tampa can be obtained at transportation hubs like Tampa International Airport, where kiosks and information desks offer complimentary guides. Many local businesses, including bike rental shops and tour operators, distribute area maps to help tourists navigate easily. The Hillsborough Area Regional Transit (HART) office provides transit maps detailing bus and streetcar routes, ideal for those relying on public transport. Additionally, museums and cultural centers often have area-specific maps featuring walking trails, historic landmarks, and must-see attractions.

Digital Maps and Navigation Apps: For travelers who prefer digital convenience, Tampa's map resources extend to a wide range of mobile applications and online platforms. Google Maps and Apple Maps provide real-time navigation, offering directions for walking, driving, cycling, and public transit. The City of Tampa's official website also hosts interactive maps that display parks, landmarks, and event locations. Apps such as Waze are particularly useful for avoiding traffic congestion, while the Tampa Riverwalk app includes a detailed waterfront navigation guide.

How to Access Tampa Maps Digitally: Visitors can access Tampa's comprehensive digital maps through various means, ensuring they are never lost while exploring the city. Clicking on the link or scanning the QR code provided in this book will take you directly to an interactive, up-to-date map of Tampa.

This digital resource allows users to zoom into specific districts, search for attractions, and even plan walking or biking routes with ease. Downloadable PDFs of Tampa's official tourism maps are also available through Visit Tampa Bay's website, allowing travelers to access them offline on their mobile devices.

GPS and Real-Time Navigation in Tampa: For those driving or using rideshare services, GPS navigation tools like Google Maps and Apple Maps provide turn-by-turn directions. Tampa's well-developed road network is easy to navigate, with clear signage directing visitors to popular destinations. Car rental companies often equip vehicles with GPS systems, making road trips around the Tampa Bay area effortless. Parking availability can also be checked in real-time using apps like ParkMobile, helping travelers find convenient spots in busy downtown areas.

Public Transportation Maps and Digital Access: Visitors relying on public transit can access HART bus and TECO Line Streetcar maps digitally through the HART website and mobile apps. These resources display schedules, fares, and stop locations, ensuring hassle-free navigation. The Pirate Water Taxi service also provides online maps indicating docking points along Tampa's waterfront, perfect for those exploring the city by boat. With the availability of transit apps, travelers can receive real-time updates on arrival times and service changes.

Navigating Tampa's Walking and Cycling Routes: For those exploring Tampa on foot or by bike, digital maps offer tailored routes through pedestrian-friendly areas like the Tampa Riverwalk and Bayshore Boulevard. The Tampa Downtown Partnership website features walking tour maps highlighting historic sites, public art installations, and cultural districts. Cyclists can use apps such as Ride with GPS to find designated bike lanes and scenic trails throughout the city. Many bike rental stations also feature QR codes that provide access to cycling route maps.

A Seamless Navigation Experience for Every Traveler: Tampa's combination of traditional and digital mapping resources ensures that every visitor, regardless of preference, can navigate the city with confidence. Whether picking up a paper map at a visitor center, using a GPS app for driving directions, or scanning a QR code for an interactive city guide, travelers have multiple options at their fingertips. By utilizing these tools, exploring Tampa becomes a stress-free and enjoyable experience, allowing visitors to focus on discovering the charm and beauty of the city.

5.2 Three to Five Days Itinerary

Embarking on a five-day journey through Tampa offers a delightful blend of history, culture, gastronomy, and natural beauty. This itinerary is crafted to provide an immersive experience, ensuring each day is filled with memorable adventures.

Day One - Immersing in Tampa's Historic Charm: Begin your exploration in Ybor City, Tampa's historic Latin Quarter. Stroll along its brick-lined streets, visiting the Ybor City Museum State Park to delve into the area's rich cigar-making heritage. For lunch, savor authentic Cuban cuisine at the Columbia Restaurant, where dishes like the "1905 Salad" and traditional paella await, with meals averaging $20-$30 per person. In the afternoon, take a guided walking tour to appreciate the district's unique architecture and vibrant murals. As evening approaches, enjoy live music at one of the local venues, immersing yourself in the lively atmosphere that defines Ybor City.

Day Two - Cultural Exploration and Culinary Delights: Start your day at the Tampa Museum of Art, located along the scenic Riverwalk. The museum showcases a diverse collection, from ancient artifacts to contemporary masterpieces. Afterward, take a leisurely walk to Armature Works, a revitalized mixed-use space featuring the Heights Public Market. Here, you can sample a variety of cuisines, from fresh seafood to artisanal pizzas, with lunch options ranging from $10-$20. In the evening, consider attending a performance at the Straz Center for the Performing Arts, where Broadway shows and local productions grace the stage, offering a taste of Tampa's vibrant arts scene.

Day Three - Nature and Relaxation: Dedicate this day to exploring Tampa's natural beauty. Visit Lettuce Lake Park, a serene haven offering boardwalks through cypress swamps and opportunities for bird-watching. Rent a kayak for a peaceful paddle along the Hillsborough River, with rentals typically costing around $25 per hour. For lunch, pack a picnic to enjoy amidst the park's tranquil surroundings. In the afternoon, head to Bayshore Boulevard, known for its scenic views of the bay and the world's longest continuous sidewalk, perfect for a leisurely bike ride or stroll. Conclude your day with a relaxing dinner at a waterfront restaurant, such as Ulele, where indigenous-inspired dishes are served, with entrees priced between $20-$35.

Day Four - Day Trip to Clearwater Beach: Take a short drive to Clearwater Beach, renowned for its pristine white sands and clear Gulf waters. Spend the morning lounging on the beach or engaging in water activities like paddleboarding or jet skiing, with rentals available on-site. For lunch, dine at Frenchy's Rockaway Grill, a local favorite offering fresh seafood with entrees around $15-$25. At noon, visit the Clearwater Marine Aquarium to learn about marine life deliverance sweat and meet Winter the dolphin, star of the "Dolphin Tale" flicks. Return to Tampa in the evening, perhaps catching a sunset along the way, and enjoy a casual dinner at a local eatery.

Day Five - Wine Tasting and Local Experiences: Conclude your trip with a visit to a local winery, such as the Florida Orange Groves Winery, where you can sample unique citrus-based wines. Tastings are often complimentary or have a nominal fee, and provide insight into Florida's fruit wine industry. For lunch, explore the Hyde Park Village, an open-air shopping district with a variety of dining options, from casual cafes to upscale restaurants, with meals averaging $15-$30. In the afternoon, consider visiting the Tampa Bay History Center to gain a deeper understanding of the region's past. As your journey comes to an end, enjoy a farewell dinner at a local restaurant, reflecting on the diverse experiences that have made your Tampa adventure unforgettable. This itinerary offers a comprehensive exploration of Tampa's multifaceted appeal, ensuring a well-rounded and enriching five-day experience.

5.3 Essential Packing List

Tampa is a city where sunshine, coastal breezes, and vibrant city life come together to create the perfect travel experience. Packing the right essentials ensures that visitors are prepared for the warm weather, outdoor adventures, and exciting urban attractions that Tampa has to offer.

Light and Comfortable Clothing: The subtropical climate of Tampa means warm temperatures for most of the year, making lightweight, breathable clothing essential. Cotton and linen fabrics are ideal for staying cool while exploring the city, whether visiting historic Ybor City or strolling along the Tampa Riverwalk. A mix of casual outfits for the day and slightly dressier attire for fine dining or nightlife will keep visitors comfortable in every setting. The humidity levels can be high, especially in summer, so packing moisture-wicking clothing helps with comfort. Having a light sweater or jacket is also useful for cooler evenings or indoor venues with strong air conditioning.

Sun Protection and Accessories: Tampa's abundant sunshine calls for strong sun protection to avoid burns and skin damage while enjoying the outdoors. A broad-spectrum sunscreen with SPF 30 or higher is a must, especially for those planning to spend time at the beach, on a boat tour, or in one of the city's many parks. A wide-brimmed hat or a comfortable cap provides additional shade and helps keep the heat at bay during long days of sightseeing. Sunglasses with UV protection are equally important to shield the eyes from the bright Florida sun. A reusable water bottle is a great addition to stay hydrated throughout the day, particularly when exploring outdoor attractions like Busch Gardens or Lettuce Lake Park.

Swimwear and Beach Essentials: With its close proximity to some of Florida's most stunning beaches, visitors should pack swimwear for a refreshing dip in the Gulf of Mexico. A quick-dry beach towel is useful for sunbathing or drying off after a swim at nearby destinations like Clearwater Beach or Fort De Soto Park. Flip-flops or water shoes make it easy to transition from the beach to casual eateries or boardwalk strolls. A waterproof phone case is helpful for those who plan to capture scenic moments while paddleboarding or boating along Tampa's waterways. Packing a beach bag with essentials like sunscreen, snacks, and an extra swimsuit ensures a seamless beach day experience.

Footwear for Every Activity: Tampa offers a variety of activities, from walking through historic districts to hiking in natural parks, making the right footwear essential. Comfortable walking shoes or sneakers are necessary for long days spent exploring attractions like the Tampa Museum of Art or the Florida Aquarium. Sandals or breathable slip-ons work well for casual outings and relaxed waterfront dining. If engaging in more adventurous activities like kayaking, biking, or zip-lining, sturdy outdoor shoes provide extra comfort and grip. Packing a pair of dressier shoes is useful for evenings out at upscale restaurants or cultural events in the city.

Travel Gadgets and Electronics: Staying connected and capturing memories requires bringing the right tech essentials for a Tampa trip. A fully charged power bank ensures that smartphones and other devices stay operational during long days of sightseeing. A high-quality camera or a smartphone with an excellent camera is perfect for capturing the stunning sunsets over Tampa Bay or the unique architecture of the city. Noise-canceling headphones come in handy for flights or relaxing moments at the hotel. Those relying on digital maps and travel apps should ensure they have mobile data or access to WiFi hotspots throughout the city.

Toiletries and Health Essentials: The combination of warm weather and outdoor activities means that visitors should pack toiletries suited for Tampa's climate. A lightweight moisturizer and lip balm with SPF help protect the skin from sun exposure and humidity. A travel-sized first aid kit with essentials like band-aids, antiseptic wipes, and pain relievers can be useful for minor injuries or headaches. Bug spray is highly recommended for visitors spending time in nature reserves or by the water during the evening. Those with specific medications should carry enough for their trip, along with copies of prescriptions if needed.

Weather-Prepared Items: While Tampa is known for its sunshine, occasional rain showers and storms can occur, particularly in the summer months. A compact, travel-friendly umbrella or a lightweight rain jacket ensures that plans aren't disrupted by sudden rainfall. Quick-dry clothing and waterproof bags are great additions for those exploring outdoor markets, amusement parks, or nature trails. Checking the weather forecast before departure helps travelers prepare appropriately for any unexpected climate shifts.

Documents and Travel Essentials: Ensuring that all necessary documents are packed in an organized and secure way makes traveling to Tampa smooth and stress-free. A valid ID or passport is required for flights, and having printed or digital copies of hotel reservations and tour confirmations is helpful. Credit and debit cards should be accompanied by some cash for small purchases at markets or food stalls. For those renting a car, a driver's license and any required insurance documents should be easily accessible. Travelers should also carry a small travel wallet or pouch to keep important documents safe while exploring.

An Effortless and Enjoyable Experience: Packing the right items for a trip to Tampa ensures that visitors can fully embrace the city's vibrant energy, outdoor beauty, and cultural experiences. From comfortable clothing to essential gadgets and health necessities, being prepared allows travelers to focus on making memories rather than worrying about forgotten items. With the right gear in hand, Tampa's dynamic mix of urban excitement and coastal relaxation awaits, promising an unforgettable journey.

5.4 Setting Your Travel Budget

Planning a trip to Tampa requires careful budgeting to ensure you get the most out of your experience without overspending. With its mix of luxury and budget-friendly options, Tampa offers a wide range of accommodations, dining, entertainment, and transportation choices. Setting a realistic budget will help you navigate your trip with ease, allowing you to enjoy everything from waterfront dining to thrilling attractions. Whether you're traveling solo, as a couple, or with family, knowing how much to allocate for each expense will make your visit smooth and enjoyable. By planning ahead, you can experience the best of Tampa while staying within your financial limits.

Accommodation Costs and Budgeting for Your Stay: Tampa provides a diverse selection of accommodations, from luxury resorts to budget hotels and vacation rentals. High-end hotels, such as the JW Marriott Tampa Water Street, can cost anywhere from $250 to $400 per night, offering premium services and waterfront views. Mid-range hotels, including Holiday Inn and Hampton Inn, typically range between $120 and $200 per night, providing comfort at a reasonable price. Budget travelers can find affordable motels and Airbnb rentals for as low as $70 to $100 per night, depending on location and availability. Booking in advance can help you secure better rates, especially during peak tourist seasons. Whether you opt for a five-star experience or a budget-friendly stay, Tampa has accommodation options to fit every budget.

Food and Dining Expenses to Consider: Tampa is known for its vibrant food scene, offering everything from fresh seafood to authentic Cuban cuisine. Fine dining restaurants, such as Bern's Steak House, charge around $75 per person for a full-course meal with drinks. Mid-range restaurants, like Ulele or Columbia Restaurant, typically cost between $25 and $50 per person for a quality meal. Budget travelers can enjoy local food trucks and casual eateries for as little as $10 to $20 per meal. Grocery shopping and preparing meals in a rental or hotel suite can also be a cost-effective alternative. Setting aside a daily food budget of $40 to $70 per person allows you to experience Tampa's culinary scene without overspending.

Transportation Costs and Getting Around the City: Tampa is a well-connected city with multiple transportation options that cater to different budgets. Renting a car costs around $30 to $60 per day, depending on the vehicle type and rental duration. Public transportation, including HART buses and the TECO Streetcar, offers affordable travel, with fares as low as $2 per ride or $5 for a day pass. Ride-sharing services like Uber and Lyft are widely available, with short trips averaging $10 to $20. Biking and walking are also great ways to explore Tampa's downtown and Riverwalk areas for free. Factoring in at least $15 to $50 per day for transportation ensures flexibility in navigating the city efficiently.

Attraction and Entertainment Expenses: Tampa offers a variety of attractions that cater to different interests and budgets, from theme parks to cultural landmarks. Busch Gardens, a top attraction, costs around $90 per person for a single-day ticket, with discounted packages available. The Florida Aquarium and ZooTampa at Lowry Park each have admission fees ranging from $35 to $45 per adult. Museums, including the Tampa Museum of Art and the Tampa Bay History Center, charge entrance fees between $10 and $20. Free activities, such as visiting the Tampa Riverwalk, exploring Ybor City, and relaxing at Clearwater Beach, help balance out entertainment expenses. Setting aside $50 to $100 per day for activities allows you to enjoy Tampa's attractions without financial strain.

Shopping and Souvenir Budgeting: Tampa's shopping scene ranges from luxury boutiques to local markets, offering something for every traveler. Hyde Park Village and International Plaza cater to high-end shoppers, where designer brands come with premium price tags. Local markets, such as the Ybor City Saturday Market, offer affordable souvenirs, handcrafted goods, and Cuban-inspired gifts. Setting a budget of $50 to $150 for shopping ensures you can purchase meaningful keepsakes without overspending. Whether you're looking for stylish clothing, handcrafted jewelry, or local art, Tampa offers plenty of shopping experiences to explore.

Emergency and Miscellaneous Expenses: Unexpected expenses can arise during any trip, making it essential to set aside extra funds for emergencies. Medical costs, lost items, or last-minute changes to travel plans can impact your budget if not planned for. Travel insurance typically costs around $50 to $100 for a short trip and can provide coverage for unforeseen events. Additional expenses, such as tipping service staff, laundry services, or minor travel add-ons, should also be considered. Having an extra $100 to $200 set aside for miscellaneous expenses ensures financial peace of mind throughout your trip.

Creating a Realistic and Flexible Travel Budget: Setting a travel budget for Tampa should be a balance between planned expenses and unexpected costs. A budget-friendly traveler can expect to spend around $100 to $150 per day, while a mid-range traveler may need between $200 and $300 daily. Luxury travelers, who enjoy high-end accommodations, dining, and exclusive experiences, should allocate at least $400 per day. By outlining daily expenses, tracking spending, and making cost-effective choices, travelers can enjoy everything Tampa has to offer while staying within budget. Careful planning allows for an unforgettable experience without financial stress.

5.5 Visa Requirements and Entry Procedures
Traveling to Tampa, Florida, offers a blend of cultural experiences, beautiful landscapes, and vibrant city life. To ensure a smooth journey, it's essential to understand the visa requirements and entry procedures, whether arriving by air, train, or road.

Visa Requirements for Nigerian Citizens: Nigerian citizens planning to visit Tampa must obtain a U.S. visa prior to their trip. The most common visa for tourism or business purposes is the B1/B2 visa. Applicants need to complete the DS-160 form online and pay the application fee, which is currently $185. Required documents include a valid Nigerian passport with at least six months' validity beyond the intended stay, a recent photograph meeting U.S. visa specifications, proof of financial stability, and evidence of strong ties to Nigeria to demonstrate intent to return after the visit. Scheduling and attending an interview at the United States Embassy or Consulate in Nigeria is a crucial part of the process. It's judicious to apply well in advance, as processing times can vary.

Entry Procedures by Air Travel: Most international visitors arrive in Tampa via Tampa International Airport (TPA). Upon landing, passengers proceed to immigration control, where they present their passport, visa, and completed customs declaration form. After clearing immigration, travelers collect their luggage from the baggage claim area on Level 1 of the Main Terminal. Following baggage retrieval, passengers go through customs inspection. For ground transportation, options include rental cars, ride-sharing services, taxis, and public transportation, all accessible from the terminal. The airport's signage is clear, and staff are available to assist newcomers.

Entry Procedures by Train: For those entering Tampa by train, Amtrak's Silver Star service stops at Tampa Union Station, located at 601 North Nebraska Avenue. While international train travel directly into Tampa is uncommon, travelers from other U.S. cities might use this mode of transportation. Upon arrival, passengers disembark and can access various ground transportation options, including taxis, ride-sharing services, and local buses. It's important to note that train stations do not have customs facilities; therefore, this mode is typically used by domestic travelers or those who have already cleared U.S. customs elsewhere.

Entry Procedures by Road: Traveling to Tampa by road involves entering the United States through a land border crossing if coming from neighboring countries. At the border, travelers must present valid travel documents, including a passport and visa. Customs and Border Protection (CBP) officers may conduct inspections and ask questions regarding the purpose of the visit. Once cleared, visitors can continue their journey to Tampa via the extensive interstate highway system. Major routes leading into Tampa include Interstate 75 and Interstate 4. It's advisable to be aware of the specific entry requirements at the chosen border crossing point, as procedures can vary.

Additional Considerations: Regardless of the mode of entry, it's essential to carry all necessary travel documents and be prepared for inspections by U.S. authorities. Familiarizing oneself with the specific procedures at the port of entry can help alleviate potential challenges. Additionally, being aware of the items prohibited or restricted by U.S. customs can prevent delays. For the most current information, consulting official U.S. government websites or contacting the U.S. Embassy or Consulate is recommended. By understanding these visa requirements and entry procedures, travelers can ensure a seamless and enjoyable visit to Tampa, ready to explore all the city has to offer.

5.6 Safety Tips and Emergency Contacts

Ensuring your safety during a visit to Tampa involves being aware of potential risks and familiarizing yourself with essential emergency contacts. By staying informed and prepared, you can enjoy a secure and pleasant experience in the city.

Emergency Services: Dial 911: In any life-threatening situation, dialing 911 connects you to police, fire, or medical services. This number is universally recognized for emergencies and should be used when immediate assistance is required. Operators are trained to handle various crises and will dispatch the appropriate responders to your location promptly. It's crucial to provide clear and concise information to ensure a swift response.

Non-Emergency Police Assistance: For non-urgent matters requiring police attention, such as reporting minor accidents or suspicious activities, contact the Tampa Police Department's non-emergency line at (813) 231-6130. This service operates 24/7, allowing residents and visitors to report concerns that do not pose an immediate threat. Utilizing this line helps keep emergency services available for critical situations.

Fire and Rescue Services: In the event of a fire or medical emergency, Tampa Fire Rescue can be reached through the 911 system. For non-emergency inquiries or information, you can contact their administrative offices at (813) 274-7011 during regular business hours. They provide fire prevention education, safety inspections, and other community services aimed at enhancing public safety.

Medical Emergencies and Poison Control: For medical emergencies, dialing 911 will summon immediate assistance. In cases of poisoning or exposure to toxic substances, the Florida Poison Information Center can be reached at 1-800-222-1222. This hotline operates 24/7, offering expert guidance on managing poison-related emergencies until professional help arrives. It's advisable to store this number in your phone for quick access.

Utility Emergencies: To report power outages or downed power lines, contact Tampa Electric Company (TECO) at 1-877-588-1010. For water-related emergencies, such as main breaks or service disruptions, the City of Tampa Water Department can be reached at (813) 274-8811. Prompt reporting of utility issues helps ensure rapid repairs and maintains public safety.

Weather-Related Emergencies: Tampa is susceptible to severe weather events, including hurricanes and tropical storms. Stay abreast with local news and weather updates. The City of Tampa's Emergency Management Office provides resources and alerts during such events. In case of a hurricane threat, visitors may be asked to evacuate waterfront areas temporarily for safety reasons. It's essential to follow official guidance and have an emergency plan in place.

General Safety Tips: While Tampa is generally safe, it's wise to remain vigilant, especially in unfamiliar areas. Stick to well-lit, populated places, particularly at night, and be cautious when exploring alone. Keep personal belongings secure and be aware of your surroundings to prevent petty theft. Familiarizing yourself with local customs and regulations can also enhance your safety during your visit. By acquainting yourself with these emergency contacts and adhering to safety guidelines, you can navigate Tampa confidently, knowing that assistance is readily available should the need arise. Preparation and awareness are key components of a safe and enjoyable stay in the city.

5.7 Currency Exchange and Banking Services

When visiting Tampa, understanding the local currency and available banking services is essential for a seamless financial experience. The United States dollar (USD) is the official currency, and visitors will find numerous facilities to manage their financial transactions efficiently.

Florida Currency Exchange: Located at 250 Westshore Plaza, Florida Currency Exchange offers a convenient option for travelers needing to convert foreign currencies. They provide competitive rates and a variety of currencies to meet diverse needs. The exchange process is straightforward, and the staff is known for their helpfulness. Operating hours are typically from 12:00 PM to 7:00 PM, Monday through Saturday, ensuring accessibility for most travelers.

Spot Currency Exchange: Situated just outside Tampa in Brandon, Spot Currency Exchange is recognized for offering some of the lowest rates around. Their expertise in foreign currency exchange markets ensures that clients receive value for their money. The location is convenient for those traveling through the area, and the service is both quick and reliable. It's advisable to check their current rates and operating hours before visiting.

The Bank of Tampa: As one of the largest independently-owned banks in the Tampa Bay Area, The Bank of Tampa provides a comprehensive range of financial services. They offer international banking services, including foreign exchange and collections, as well as foreign remittance and money transfers. Their commitment to personalized service makes them a reliable choice for visitors seeking banking assistance. Branches are conveniently located throughout the city, with standard banking hours on weekdays.

Fifth Third Bank: With multiple branches in Tampa, including the Tampa Main branch at 201 East Kennedy Boulevard, Fifth Third Bank offers personal, small business, and commercial banking solutions. They provide services such as checking and savings accounts, credit cards, and online banking. For visitors, Fifth Third Bank's extensive ATM network and customer service can be particularly useful. It's recommended to check their specific services and hours of operation before visiting.

Suncoast Credit Union: Serving the Tampa area, Suncoast Credit Union offers a range of financial services, including savings and checking accounts, loans, and online banking. As a credit union, they often provide favorable rates and personalized service. Visitors can access their services at various branches, with the South Manhattan Avenue branch being a convenient option. It's advisable to review their membership requirements and services to determine suitability. When exchanging currency, it's prudent to compare rates and fees among different providers to ensure the best value. Additionally, many establishments in Tampa accept major credit and debit cards, which can offer favorable exchange rates and added convenience. However, having some local currency on hand is advisable for small purchases or in situations where cards may not be accepted. By familiarizing yourself with these banking services and currency exchange options, you can manage your finances effectively during your stay in Tampa.

5.8 Language, Communication and Useful Phrases

Tampa is a vibrant city where cultures blend seamlessly, creating a unique linguistic and social atmosphere. As part of Florida, English is the primary language spoken, but Spanish also plays a significant role due to the city's rich Latin American and Cuban heritage. Whether exploring the historic streets of Ybor City, dining at a waterfront restaurant, or interacting with locals, understanding the nuances of communication in Tampa enhances the experience. Travelers will find that a mix of formal and casual expressions makes conversations smooth and enjoyable.

English as the Primary Language: English is widely spoken in Tampa, and most services, businesses, and attractions operate in English. Visitors who speak English will find it easy to communicate in hotels, restaurants, and shopping centers. Public transportation, signs, and tourist information are all provided in English, ensuring accessibility for international travelers. While the local dialect is generally neutral, some Floridian and Southern expressions may appear in casual conversations. Words like "y'all" (you all) and "bless your heart" (an expression with varying meanings) may be commonly heard in friendly exchanges.

The Influence of Spanish in Tampa: Due to Tampa's deep-rooted Cuban, Puerto Rican, and Latin American influences, Spanish is the second most commonly spoken language. Many residents, particularly in Ybor City and West Tampa, speak Spanish fluently, and some businesses operate in both English and Spanish. Street names, restaurant menus, and local events often include Spanish influences, reflecting the city's diverse cultural heritage. Travelers who speak or understand basic Spanish may find it helpful in certain neighborhoods and when interacting with Spanish-speaking locals. Even those who do not speak Spanish will notice its presence in everyday conversations and signage around the city.

Commonly Used English Phrases in Tampa: For travelers unfamiliar with American English, learning a few commonly used phrases can be helpful in navigating the city. Everyday greetings like "Hey," "Good morning, how are you?" and "Hi, what's up?" are polite ways to start conversations. When asking for directions, say "Where is the closest bus stop?" or "Can you recommend a good restaurant?" are practical. In restaurants, asking for the check with "Can I get the bill, please?" or ordering by saying "I'll have the…" makes dining experiences smoother. Understanding responses like "Take care," "Have a good one," and "You're welcome" helps with everyday interactions.

Spanish Phrases That Are Useful in Tampa: Visitors who wish to engage more deeply with the local culture can benefit from learning a few Spanish phrases. Basic greetings such as "Hola" (Hello) and "Buenos días" (Good morning) are commonly used, especially in Hispanic neighborhoods. When dining, phrases like "Una mesa para dos, por favor" (A table for two, please) and "Gracias" (Thank you) show courtesy. If seeking assistance, asking "¿Dónde está…?" (Where is…?) can be useful. Even if not fluent, making an effort to speak Spanish is often appreciated by the locals and can enhance cultural connections.

Non-Verbal Communication in Tampa: Beyond language, non-verbal communication plays an essential role in interactions throughout Tampa. A friendly smile and maintaining eye contact are signs of politeness and engagement in conversations. Handshakes are common in business settings, while casual conversations may involve more relaxed gestures. In social settings, nodding while listening indicates attentiveness and agreement. While Tampa has a generally warm and welcoming culture, respecting personal space and avoiding overly direct gestures helps maintain positive interactions.

Navigating Signs and Public Announcements: Throughout Tampa, visitors will find signs and public announcements primarily in English, with some bilingual signage in Spanish. In transportation hubs like Tampa International Airport and Union Station, important information is displayed in both languages for accessibility. Restaurants, museums, and tourist attractions often provide English-Spanish translations to accommodate diverse visitors. Public service announcements, such as weather alerts and emergency information, are primarily in English but may also include Spanish translations. Recognizing key words like "Exit," "Restroom," and "No Smoking" ensures smooth navigation in public spaces.

Cultural Etiquette in Communication: Tampa's diverse population means that social interactions often reflect a blend of cultures, making politeness and friendliness key aspects of communication. Saying "please" and "thank you" is expected in everyday conversations, whether ordering food or asking for directions. Holding the door open for others and using phrases like "Excuse me" or "Sorry" in crowded spaces reflects good manners. Tipping is customary in restaurants, with 15-20% considered standard for good service. Engaging in small talk about the weather, sports, or local events is common when interacting with locals.

Adapting to Tampa's Communication Style: Visitors will quickly notice that Tampa's communication style is friendly, casual, and accommodating, making it easy to interact with both locals and service providers. While business settings may require a more formal tone, most social interactions are relaxed and welcoming. Asking for recommendations, whether for dining, entertainment, or outdoor activities, is a great way to connect with residents. Travelers who show curiosity about Tampa's culture and history will often find locals eager to share insights and personal experiences. Whether speaking English or using a few Spanish phrases, embracing the city's linguistic diversity enriches the travel experience.

5.9 Shopping in Tampa

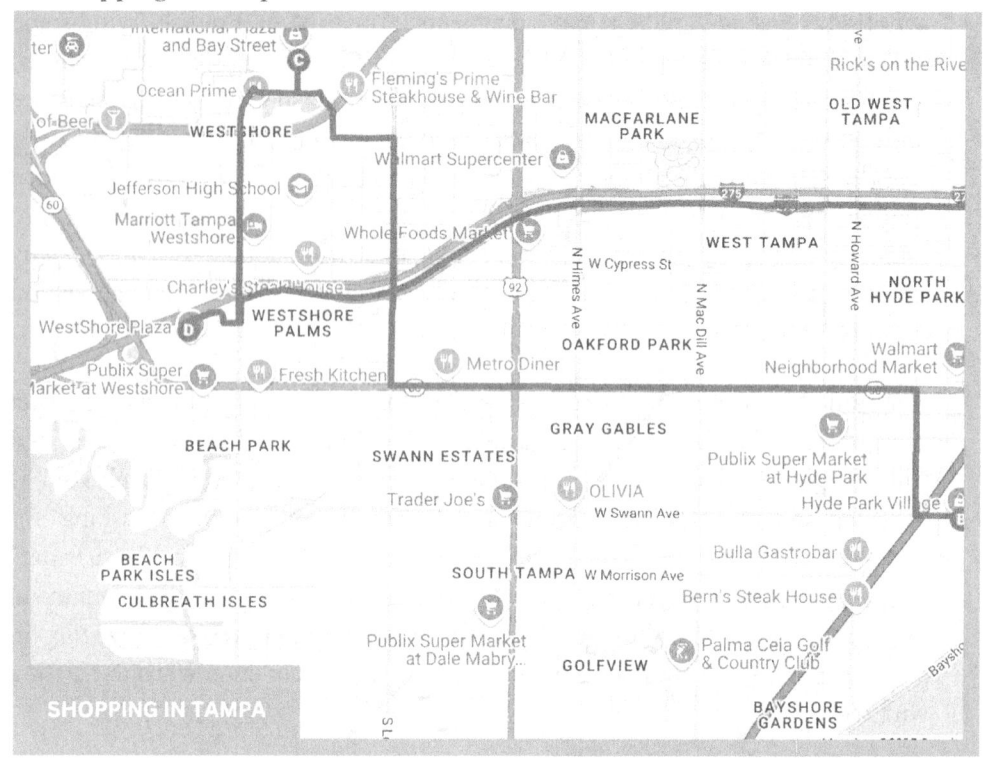

Directions from Tampa, FL, USA to Ybor City Historic District, Tampa, FL, USA

A
Tampa, FL, USA

D
WestShore Plaza, Westshore Plaza, Tampa, FL, USA

B
Hyde Park Village, West Swann Avenue, Tampa, FL, USA

E
Tampa Premium Outlets, Grand Cypress Drive, Lutz, FL, USA

C
International Plaza and Bay Street, North Westshore Boulevard, Tampa, FL, USA

F
Ybor City Historic District, Tampa, FL, USA

Tampa offers a diverse shopping experience, with several distinct districts catering to various tastes and preferences. Each area provides a unique blend of retail options, dining, and entertainment, ensuring that visitors find exactly what they're looking for.

Hyde Park Village: Located in the historic Hyde Park neighborhood, Hyde Park Village is an upscale open-air shopping district. Spanning six city blocks, it features a mix of national retailers like Anthropologie and Pottery Barn, as well as local boutiques and restaurants. Visitors can enjoy a leisurely shopping experience amidst tree-lined streets and charming architecture. The village also hosts events such as fresh markets and fitness classes, enhancing its community appeal.

International Plaza and Bay Street: Situated near Tampa International Airport, International Plaza and Bay Street is a premier shopping destination. The mall boasts over 200 specialty stores, including high-end retailers like Neiman Marcus, Nordstrom, and Louis Vuitton. Bay Street, an adjacent open-air village, offers a variety of dining and nightlife options, making it a vibrant spot for both shopping and entertainment. Its proximity to the airport makes it easily accessible for travelers.

WestShore Plaza: Located at the intersection of West Shore and Kennedy Boulevards, WestShore Plaza is a convenient shopping center for both locals and visitors. Anchored by major department stores like Macy's and JCPenney, it offers a variety of retail options. The plaza also features a selection of restaurants and a movie theater, providing a comprehensive shopping and entertainment experience. The location is ideal, allowing for easy access from multiple areas of the city.

Tampa Premium Outlets: Located in Lutz, just north of Tampa, Tampa Premium Outlets is a haven for bargain hunters. The center features over 110 stores, including popular brands like Michael Kors, Adidas, and Coach, offering discounted prices. The open-air mall is designed with a Key West theme, providing a pleasant shopping atmosphere. Ample parking and a variety of dining options make it a convenient destination for a day of shopping.

Ybor City: Ybor City, Tampa's historic Latin Quarter, offers a unique shopping experience with its eclectic mix of boutiques, vintage shops, and specialty stores. Known for its rich cultural heritage, the district features cobblestone streets and historic architecture. Visitors can explore cigar shops, art galleries, and unique clothing stores, all reflecting the area's diverse cultural influences. The district is easily accessible via the TECO Line Streetcar, adding to its charm.

SoHo District: Short for "South Howard," the SoHo District is a trendy area known for its chic boutiques and vibrant nightlife. Along South Howard Avenue, shoppers will find a variety of fashion-forward stores offering unique apparel and accessories. The district also boasts an array of restaurants and bars, making it a popular destination for both shopping and evening entertainment. Its proximity to Hyde Park adds to its appeal, creating a dynamic shopping corridor. Each of these districts contributes to Tampa's dynamic retail landscape, ensuring that visitors have access to a wide range of shopping experiences. Whether you're seeking luxury brands, local crafts, or unique finds, Tampa's shopping districts offer something for every shopper.

5.10 Health and Wellness Centers

Tampa offers a variety of health and wellness centers catering to diverse needs, ensuring visitors can find the perfect place to rejuvenate during their stay. Whether looking for relaxation, holistic care, or medical wellness treatments, the city offers top-tier services that enhance overall well-being. From advanced therapies to traditional spa experiences, these wellness centers provide high-quality care and specialized treatments for every visitor.

Health and Glow: Located at 4331 S Manhattan Ave, Tampa, FL 33611, Health and Glow blends primary care with high-end med spa services. This center offers IV therapy, weight loss programs, hormone optimization, and aesthetic treatments designed to restore energy and boost overall wellness. Visitors can book personalized health consultations or indulge in revitalizing skincare services for a complete wellness experience. Prices vary depending on treatments, with IV therapy starting at $99 and other aesthetic services available upon consultation. Appointments can be scheduled online at myhealthandglow.com, and the facility is easily accessible by car or public transportation.

Tao Wellness Med Spa: Located in the heart of Tampa at 2001 W Kennedy Blvd, Tampa, FL 33606, Tao Wellness Med Spa provides a tranquil escape with state-of-the-art wellness treatments. The spa specializes in medical-grade facials, injectables, deep tissue massages, and holistic therapies designed to promote relaxation and rejuvenation. Their expert staff tailors each service to meet individual health and skincare goals, ensuring a transformative experience for every visitor. Pricing varies, with facials starting at $150 and therapeutic massages at $120. Guests can book appointments through their website at taowellnessmedspa.com, and the spa is conveniently located near major Tampa landmarks.

Tampa Bay Holistic Wellness: For visitors seeking a more integrative and natural approach to health, Tampa Bay Holistic Wellness provides specialized care with a focus on functional medicine. Situated at 1205 N Franklin St. Suite 100, Tampa, FL 33602, this center emphasizes identifying the root causes of health concerns and treating them through a combination of naturopathic and modern medical techniques. Services include acupuncture, nutritional counseling, detox programs, and hormone balancing therapies, helping clients achieve optimal well-being. Treatment prices range from $80 for acupuncture sessions to $250 for in-depth health consultations. Visitors can schedule an appointment online at tampabayholisticwellness.com and easily access the facility by car or rideshare.

Envizion Medical: Envizion Medical, located at 2711 Letap Ct, Suite 101, Land O' Lakes, FL 34638, specializes in hormone replacement therapy, medical weight loss, and regenerative treatments. This center is highly recommended for those looking to enhance energy levels, improve metabolic health, and regain youthful vitality through cutting-edge therapies. Services include testosterone replacement therapy, peptide therapy, and customized weight loss programs tailored to individual health needs. Prices start at $99 for consultations, with specialized treatments available upon request. The clinic is a short drive from central Tampa, and visitors can learn more or book an appointment at envizionmedical.com.

Tampa Bay Total Wellness: Tampa Bay Total Wellness offers a full spectrum of health services, from advanced aesthetic procedures to bio-identical hormone therapy. Conveniently located in Tampa, this wellness center provides expert-led treatments designed to optimize both physical and mental well-being. Services include body contouring, IV nutrient therapy, and anti-aging treatments that promote longevity and vitality. Prices vary based on treatment plans, with aesthetic services starting at $200 and wellness consultations at $150. Visitors can book appointments and explore services at tampabaytotalwellness.com, ensuring a personalized wellness journey tailored to their needs.

A Rejuvenating Wellness Experience in Tampa: Each of these wellness centers in Tampa offers a unique approach to health, ensuring visitors can find the right balance of relaxation, rejuvenation, and medical care. Whether in need of spa treatments, holistic therapies, or specialized medical services, these locations provide top-tier wellness solutions. With experienced practitioners, cutting-edge treatments, and a commitment to overall health, Tampa's wellness centers offer visitors a revitalizing experience during their stay.

5.11 Useful Websites, Mobile Apps and Online Resources
When visiting Tampa, leveraging local digital resources can significantly enhance your experience, providing real-time information and convenient services. Several websites and mobile applications are tailored to assist visitors in navigating the city's attractions, transportation, and events.

Visit Tampa Bay Official Website: The official tourism website, https://www.visittampabay.com/ offers comprehensive information on attractions, dining, and events. It features detailed guides to the city's neighborhoods, cultural sites, and outdoor activities. The site also provides itineraries and trip planning tools to help visitors maximize their stay. Regular updates ensure that users have access to the latest happenings in Tampa.

Coast Bike Share App: For eco-friendly transportation, the app allows users to locate and rent bicycles throughout Tampa. With numerous stations across the city, it offers a convenient way to explore areas like the Tampa Riverwalk and Bayshore Boulevard. The app provides real-time bike availability and easy payment options, making urban cycling accessible to visitors.

Pirate Water Taxi App: To experience Tampa from its scenic waterways, the https://www.piratewatertaxi.com/ app is invaluable. It offers information on routes, schedules, and ticket purchases for the water taxi service that stops at key attractions along the Hillsborough River. The app enhances the convenience of exploring the city's waterfront destinations.

UNATION App: Staying informed about local events is effortless with the https://www.unation.com/ app. It curates a comprehensive list of happenings in Tampa, from concerts and festivals to community gatherings. Users can search events by category, date, or location, ensuring they don't miss out on the city's vibrant social scene. The app also allows for ticket purchases and event reminders.

Tampa Trash and Recycling App: For practical information on waste disposal, the https://www.tampa.gov/info/mobile-applications app provides schedules, disposal guidelines, and reminders. Visitors staying in residential areas or vacation rentals can benefit from understanding local waste management practices. The app ensures users are informed about collection days and proper recycling procedures.

Hillsborough County Public Library Cooperative Mobile Apps: The https://hcplc.org/research/apps offers mobile apps that grant access to a vast collection of digital resources. Visitors can borrow eBooks, audiobooks, and access research databases during their stay. The apps also provide information on library locations, hours, and events, serving as a valuable resource for educational and recreational needs. Utilizing these digital tools can greatly enhance a visitor's experience in Tampa, offering convenience and up-to-date information at their fingertips. Whether navigating the city's attractions, staying informed about events, or accessing local services, these resources are designed to assist in making the most of your visit.

5.12 Internet Access and Connectivity

Tampa is a modern city with seamless internet connectivity, ensuring that visitors can stay connected for work, socializing, and navigation. Whether exploring the city's attractions, working remotely, or simply browsing for recommendations, Tampa offers reliable internet access through multiple providers and public Wi-Fi hotspots.

Reliable Internet Service Providers: Tampa is home to major internet service providers that deliver high-speed connectivity to businesses, hotels, and residential areas. Providers such as Spectrum, AT&T Fiber, and Xfinity offer a range of options, with fiber-optic connections available in many parts of the city. Visitors staying in hotels and vacation rentals will find that most accommodations provide free Wi-Fi with fast download speeds. Those needing high-bandwidth services for video calls or remote work can access premium internet packages at select co-working spaces and business centers. With the city's robust infrastructure, visitors rarely experience connectivity issues, making Tampa an excellent destination for digital nomads.

Public Wi-Fi Hotspots Across the City: For travelers who rely on free internet access, Tampa offers numerous public Wi-Fi hotspots throughout the city. The Tampa Riverwalk and Curtis Hixon Waterfront Park provide free high-speed internet, allowing visitors to relax while staying connected. Major transportation hubs, including Tampa International Airport and Union Station, also offer complimentary Wi-Fi for travelers in transit. Coffee shops such as Starbucks and local cafés provide free internet access, making them popular spots for remote work and casual browsing. With Wi-Fi available in libraries, museums, and shopping centers, visitors can easily check emails, use maps, or share their experiences online.

Mobile Data and Network Coverage: Visitors relying on mobile data will find strong and consistent network coverage across Tampa, with major carriers like Verizon, T-Mobile, and AT&T offering 4G and 5G connectivity. The city's urban areas, including Downtown Tampa, Ybor City, and Channelside, experience fast mobile speeds suitable for video streaming and conference calls. Travelers from abroad can purchase prepaid SIM cards at retail stores like Walmart and Best Buy, ensuring affordable and reliable mobile internet access. Those with eSIM-compatible devices can activate local data plans instantly, eliminating the need for physical SIM cards. Whether navigating city streets or exploring outdoor attractions, mobile networks in Tampa provide seamless connectivity.

Co-Working Spaces and High-Speed Internet Hubs: For business travelers and digital nomads, Tampa offers an array of co-working spaces equipped with high-speed internet and modern amenities. Locations such as Industrious Tampa, Regus, and CoCreativ provide comfortable workspaces, private offices, and conference rooms with ultra-fast internet. Many of these spaces offer daily or hourly passes, allowing visitors to work in a professional setting while in the city. Tampa's tech-friendly environment makes it an attractive destination for remote workers seeking productivity alongside beautiful scenery. With co-working hubs available across the city, finding a quiet and connected place to work is effortless.

Connectivity for Streaming, Gaming, and Entertainment: Visitors looking to stream content, play online games, or engage in high-bandwidth activities will find that Tampa's internet speeds support seamless entertainment. Hotels and short-term rentals typically provide strong Wi-Fi connections, making it easy to watch movies, download large files, or stay engaged on social media. Gaming lounges and e-sports centers in Tampa cater to visitors who enjoy online gaming with ultra-low latency networks. Public Wi-Fi hotspots and 5G mobile data ensure that entertainment is never out of reach, whether relaxing in a hotel room or exploring the city.

Staying Secure While Online: While public Wi-Fi is widely available, visitors should take precautions to secure their data while browsing in open networks. Using VPN services helps protect sensitive information and ensures a safer online experience. Many cafes and co-working spaces offer secure private networks for business travelers needing encrypted connections. Those conducting financial transactions or accessing personal data should opt for mobile data over public Wi-Fi to minimize security risks. By taking simple precautions, visitors can enjoy Tampa's digital connectivity without compromising their privacy.

A Seamless Digital Experience in Tampa: Tampa's modern infrastructure ensures that visitors can enjoy uninterrupted internet access whether they are sightseeing, working, or relaxing. With a combination of free public Wi-Fi, strong mobile networks, and co-working hubs, staying connected is effortless in this tech-friendly city. Whether sharing vacation moments online or staying productive while traveling, Tampa offers a seamless and fast digital experience for every visitor.

5.13 Visitor Centers and Tourist Assistance

Tampa offers several visitor centers to help travelers navigate the city and make the most of their stay. These centers provide maps, brochures, expert recommendations, and local insights for a seamless travel experience.

Visit Tampa Bay Visitor Center: Located in the heart of downtown, the Visit Tampa Bay Visitor Center is the go-to spot for travel advice. It offers free maps, attraction discounts, and expert recommendations on things to do in the city. For more information, visit their website at www.visittampabay.com.

Tampa International Airport Information Center: Conveniently located at Tampa International Airport, this center helps travelers upon arrival. It provides transportation details, hotel recommendations, and information on local attractions. For enquiries, visit www.tampaairport.com.

Ybor City Visitor Information Center: Located in the historic Ybor City district, this center is ideal for exploring Tampa's Cuban heritage. It offers details on local tours, cigar shops, and cultural experiences in the area. To get more information, visit www.ybor.org

Tampa Union Station Visitor Center: Housed in a historic train station, this center is perfect for those arriving by rail. It provides insights into Tampa's history, public transport options, and nearby attractions. To learn more about them, visit their website at www.tampaunionstation.com.

Florida Aquarium Guest Services: For visitors exploring marine life, the Florida Aquarium Guest Services offers ticketing help and visitor guidance. It provides accessibility services, tour details, and special event information. Located at 701 Channelside Drive, Tampa, FL 33602, guests can visit www.flaquarium.org for more details. These centers ensure visitors have all the information needed for a smooth and enjoyable experience in Tampa. Whether seeking cultural attractions, transportation guidance, or local events, expert assistance is always available.

CHAPTER 6
GASTRONOMIC DELIGHTS

6.1 Dining Options and Top Restaurants

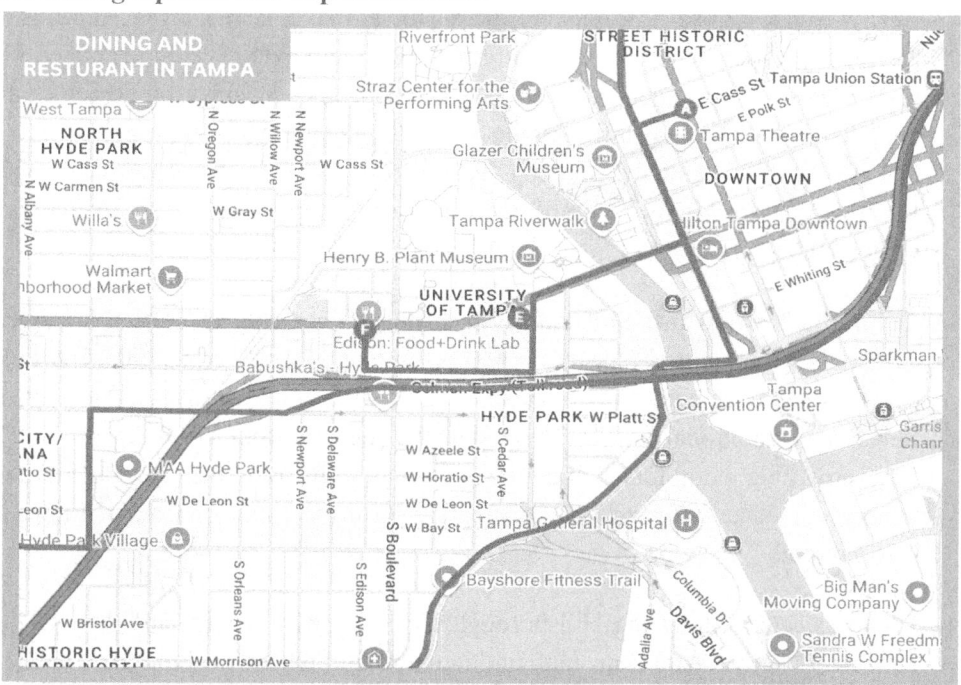

Directions from Tampa, FL, USA to Edison: Food+Drink Lab, West Kennedy Boulevard, Tampa, FL, USA

A Tampa, FL, USA	**D** Ulele, North Highland Avenue, Tampa, FL, USA
B Bern's Steak House, South Howard Avenue, Tampa, FL,* USA	**E** Oxford Exchange, West Kennedy Boulevard, Tampa, FL, USA
C Columbia Restaurant, East 7th Avenue, Tampa, FL, USA	**F** Edison: Food+Drink Lab, West Kennedy Boulevard, Tampa. FL. USA

Tampa's culinary scene offers a rich tapestry of flavors, reflecting its diverse cultural heritage. From historic establishments to modern eateries, the city provides a variety of dining options to satisfy every palate.

Bern's Steak House: Located at 1208 S Howard Ave, Bern's Steak House is a Tampa institution renowned for its prime steaks and extensive wine collection. The menu features aged steaks, fresh seafood, and an array of desserts, all complemented by an award-winning wine list. Operating hours are from 5:00 PM to 10:00 PM daily, making it an ideal spot for an elegant dinner. Reservations are highly recommended due to its popularity among locals and visitors alike.

Columbia Restaurant: Situated in the historic Ybor City at 2117 E 7th Ave, Columbia Restaurant is Florida's oldest restaurant, established in 1905. It offers authentic Spanish and Cuban cuisine, with signature dishes like the "1905 Salad" and traditional paella. The restaurant operates from 11:00 AM to 10:00 PM, providing both lunch and dinner services. Its rich history and vibrant atmosphere make it a must-visit destination for those seeking a taste of Tampa's cultural roots.

Ulele: Located along the Hillsborough River at 1810 N Highland Ave, Ulele celebrates Native American and multicultural influences on Florida's cuisine. The menu includes items like charbroiled oysters and alligator hush puppies, paired with house-brewed beers. Open from 11:00 AM to 10:00 PM, Ulele offers a unique dining experience with scenic riverfront views. Its commitment to locally sourced ingredients ensures fresh and flavorful dishes.

Oxford Exchange: Located at 420 W Kennedy Blvd, Oxford Exchange is a blend of restaurant, bookstore, and boutique, offering a unique dining and shopping experience. The menu features contemporary American cuisine, including breakfast, brunch, and lunch options like avocado toast and artisanal sandwiches. Open from 7:30 AM to 5:30 PM, it's an ideal spot for a leisurely brunch or afternoon tea. The elegant décor and inviting atmosphere make it a favorite among locals and tourists.

Edison - Food+Drink Lab: At 912 W Kennedy Blvd, Edison: Food+Drink Lab offers an innovative dining experience with a menu that changes regularly to highlight seasonal ingredients. The restaurant serves inventive dishes that blend various culinary techniques and flavors, accompanied by craft cocktails.

Operating hours are from 5:00 PM to 10:00 PM, making it a perfect choice for dinner. Its modern ambiance and creative cuisine attract food enthusiasts looking for something different.

Datz: Situated at 2616 S MacDill Ave, Datz is a lively eatery known for its hearty comfort food and extensive beer selection. The menu boasts items like the "Cheesy Todd" burger and "Barry C's Stuffed Meatloaf," offering a playful twist on classic dishes. Open from 11:00 AM to 10:00 PM, Datz provides a casual and fun dining atmosphere. Its generous portions and eclectic menu make it a popular spot for families and groups.

Each of these establishments contributes uniquely to Tampa's vibrant dining landscape, ensuring that visitors have a plethora of options to explore and enjoy during their stay.

6.2 Cafes and Bakeries

Tampa's vibrant culinary scene boasts an array of charming cafes and bakeries, each offering unique flavors and atmospheres. Exploring these establishments provides visitors with delightful experiences that capture the essence of the city.

La Segunda Central Bakery: Located in Ybor City at 2512 N 15th Street, La Segunda Central Bakery has been a Tampa staple since 1915. Renowned for its authentic Cuban bread and pastries, the bakery offers delights such as guava turnovers and traditional Cuban sandwiches. Operating hours are from 6:30 AM to 5:00 PM, Monday through Saturday, and 6:30 AM to 2:00 PM on Sundays. Visitors can savor a taste of Tampa's rich Cuban heritage in every bite. lasegundabakery.com

Alessi Bakery: Located at 2909 W Cypress Street, Alessi Bakery has been serving the Tampa community since 1912. This family-owned establishment offers a wide range of Italian and Cuban baked goods, including pastries, cookies, and custom cakes. The bakery operates from 7:00 AM to 6:00 PM, Monday through Saturday, and is closed on Sundays. Its long-standing reputation makes it a must-visit for those seeking traditional baked treats. tampabay.com

Sucré Table: Situated in the Hyde Park neighborhood at 1801 N Howard Avenue, Sucré Table is a modern patisserie known for its inventive desserts and pastries. The menu features items like macarons, tarts, and specialty cakes, all crafted with artistic flair. Open from 10:00 AM to 6:00 PM, Wednesday through Sunday, the bakery provides a contemporary twist on classic confections. authenticflorida.com

Buddy Brew Coffee: At 2020 W Kennedy Boulevard, Buddy Brew Coffee offers a haven for coffee enthusiasts. This local roastery serves freshly brewed coffees alongside a selection of pastries and light bites. Operating hours are from 7:00 AM to 6:00 PM, Monday through Friday, and 8:00 AM to 6:00 PM on weekends. The inviting atmosphere makes it an ideal spot for relaxation or casual meetings. guidedbydestiny.com

The Attic Cafe: Perched atop 500 E Kennedy Boulevard, The Attic Cafe provides a cozy setting with panoramic views of downtown Tampa. The menu includes a variety of coffees, teas, sandwiches, and baked goods, catering to both breakfast and lunch crowds. Open from 7:00 AM to 3:00 PM on weekdays, the cafe offers a serene escape amidst the urban hustle. guidedbydestiny.com

Bake'n Babes: Located within the Armature Works at 1910 N Ola Avenue, Bake'n Babes is known for its indulgent desserts and creative baked treats. Popular items include over-the-top milkshakes, cookies, and brownies, appealing to those with a sweet tooth. The bakery operates from 11:00 AM to 9:00 PM, Sunday through Thursday, and extends to 11:00 PM on Fridays and Saturdays. It's a must-visit spot for dessert enthusiasts seeking unique confections. visittampabay.com Each of these establishments contributes uniquely to Tampa's rich tapestry of flavors, offering visitors a chance to indulge in both traditional and contemporary culinary delights. Exploring these cafes and bakeries provides a delicious insight into the city's diverse gastronomic culture.

6.4 Cooking Classes and Culinary Tours

Tampa's rich culinary heritage offers visitors a chance to delve into its diverse flavors through engaging cooking classes and immersive food tours. These experiences not only showcase the city's gastronomic delights but also provide insights into its cultural tapestry.

Cozymeal Cooking Classes: Cozymeal offers a variety of cooking classes in Tampa, connecting participants with professional chefs in intimate settings. Classes cover a range of cuisines, from Italian to Asian fusion, and are held at various locations throughout the city. Sessions are typically scheduled during evenings and weekends, accommodating both locals and tourists. Participants can expect hands-on instruction, culminating in a shared meal of the dishes prepared. Booking and class details are available on their website. cozymeal.com

Tampa Bay Food Tours: For those eager to explore Tampa's culinary landscape, Tampa Bay Food Tours provides guided walking tours that highlight the city's best eateries. One of their popular offerings is the Riverwalk Dine & Wine Tour, a 3.5-hour evening excursion that visits four to five restaurants along the scenic Riverwalk. Each stop features curated tastings, with three venues offering wine pairings. Tours are scheduled regularly, and reservations can be made through their website. tampabayfoodtours.com

Epicurean Theatre at the Epicurean Hotel: Located at 1207 South Howard Avenue, the Epicurean Theatre is a culinary playground within the Epicurean Hotel. It hosts a variety of events, including cooking demonstrations, wine tastings, and mixology classes led by renowned chefs and sommeliers. The theatre's schedule varies, with events typically held in the evenings. Attendees can expect interactive sessions that blend education with entertainment. Details on upcoming events and ticket purchases are available on their website. epicureanhotel.com

Ybor City Food Tours: Ybor City Food Tours offers a three-hour walking tour through Tampa's historic Ybor City neighborhood. Participants visit several local establishments to sample dishes that reflect the area's rich cultural heritage, including Cuban, Spanish, and Italian influences. Tours are typically conducted during the day and provide both culinary tastings and historical insights.

AJ's Kitchen Drawer Cooking Classes: AJ's Kitchen Drawer provides hands-on cooking experiences led by skilled chefs. Located in the Tampa area, they offer classes that focus on creating gourmet meals from scratch, teaching participants new techniques and flavor profiles. Classes are scheduled regularly, often in the evenings, and cater to various skill levels. More information on upcoming classes and registration can be found on their website. ajskitchendrawer.com Engaging in these cooking classes and culinary tours offers visitors a deeper appreciation of Tampa's diverse food scene, blending hands-on learning with rich cultural experiences.

6.5 Traditional Floridian Cuisine

Tampa's culinary landscape is a rich tapestry woven from its diverse cultural heritage and abundant local resources. Visitors seeking an authentic Floridian dining experience will find a variety of traditional dishes that capture the essence of the region.

Cuban Sandwich: A quintessential Tampa creation, the Cuban sandwich reflects the city's rich immigrant history. Traditionally, it features Cuban bread layered with mojo-marinated roast pork, ham, Genoa salami, Swiss cheese, pickles, and mustard. The Columbia Restaurant in Ybor City, established in 1905, is renowned for its rendition of this classic. Prices typically range from $10 to $15. Nutritionally, it's a hearty meal rich in protein and fats. For an authentic experience, pair it with a side of plantain chips. columbiarestaurant.com

Deviled Crab: Originating from Tampa's Spanish and Cuban communities, deviled crab is a flavorful dish featuring crab meat mixed with spices, breaded, and deep-fried. It's commonly found in local eateries throughout Ybor City. Prices are generally around $5 to $8 per serving. This dish offers a good source of protein, though it's also high in fats due to frying. Enjoy it with a squeeze of lemon to enhance its flavors. tampamagazines.com

Grouper Sandwich: A staple in Tampa's coastal cuisine, the grouper sandwich showcases fresh, locally caught grouper, either grilled or fried, served on a bun with lettuce, tomato, and tartar sauce. The Rusty Pelican, located on the waterfront, is celebrated for its version of this dish. Expect to pay between $15 and $20. This sandwich is rich in lean protein and omega-3 fatty acids, especially when the fish is grilled. Pair it with a side of coleslaw for a balanced meal. therustypelicantampa.com

Key Lime Pie: A Floridian dessert classic, Key lime pie is made from Key lime juice, sweetened condensed milk, and a graham cracker crust, offering a sweet and tangy flavor profile. Many Tampa restaurants feature this dessert, with prices ranging from $6 to $8 per slice. While it's high in sugars and fats, it's a delightful treat to conclude a meal. For the most authentic taste, ensure the pie is made with real Key lime juice. cookingenie.com

Stone Crab Claws: In season from October to May, stone crab claws are a delicacy in Tampa, known for their sweet, tender meat. Ulele, a native-inspired restaurant along the Hillsborough River, offers fresh stone crab claws when available. Prices can be higher, often $30 or more, reflecting their delicacy status. With low fat content and high protein levels, they offer a healthy and nutritious option. Enjoy them chilled with a mustard dipping sauce for a true Floridian experience. ulele.com Exploring these traditional dishes provides a flavorful journey through Tampa's culinary heritage, offering visitors a taste of the city's diverse cultural influences and local ingredients.

6.6 Local Markets and Street Food
Tampa's culinary landscape is rich with diverse flavors, best experienced through its bustling local markets and dynamic food halls. These venues offer visitors a chance to savor a variety of cuisines, shop for unique products, and immerse themselves in the city's vibrant culture.

Heights Public Market at Armature Works: Located at 1910 N Ola Ave, Heights Public Market is a 22,000-square-foot industrial-style market hall within the historic Armature Works building. Home to over 14 local eateries, it offers a curated selection of culinary delights ranging from Asian fusion to classic BBQ. The market operates daily, typically from morning until late evening, providing ample opportunity for breakfast, lunch, or dinner. Prices vary by vendor, with options suitable for both casual snacking and more substantial meals. Visitors can enjoy communal seating areas, making it an ideal spot for groups with diverse tastes. armatureworks.com

Ybor City Saturday Market: Situated in the heart of the historic Ybor City neighborhood at Centennial Park, the Ybor City Saturday Market is a vibrant outdoor market held every Saturday from 9 AM to 3 PM. This market features a variety of vendors offering fresh produce, handcrafted goods, and local art. Prices are generally reasonable, with many unique items that make for perfect souvenirs. It's recommended to arrive early to enjoy the freshest selections and to experience the market before the midday heat. The market's lively atmosphere provides a glimpse into Tampa's rich cultural heritage.

Sparkman Wharf: Located at 615 Channelside Drive, Sparkman Wharf is an innovative outdoor food hall that combines dining, entertainment, and retail along Tampa's waterfront. The venue features a collection of shipping containers transformed into culinary kiosks, each offering a unique menu. Open daily from 11 AM to 10 PM, Sparkman Wharf provides a variety of dining options, with prices typically ranging from $10 to $20 per dish. Visitors can enjoy live music, open green spaces, and picturesque views of the harbor, making it a popular spot for both families and nightlife enthusiasts. tampabay.com

Hyde Park Village Fresh Market: On the first Sunday of each month, Hyde Park Village hosts the Fresh Market, a community event featuring local vendors, artisans, and farmers. Located in the charming Hyde Park neighborhood, the market operates from 10 AM to 3 PM, offering fresh produce, baked goods, and handcrafted items. Prices are competitive, and the quality of goods is exceptional. The market is pet-friendly and provides a relaxed atmosphere, making it a delightful way to spend a Sunday morning. visittampabay.com

The Hall on Franklin: Situated at 1701 N Franklin St, The Hall on Franklin is a collective eatery that brings together several independent restaurants under one roof. This upscale food hall offers a variety of cuisines, from gourmet coffee and pastries to sushi and Southern comfort food. Operating hours vary by vendor, but the hall generally opens from 7 AM to 10 PM, catering to both early birds and night owls. Prices are moderate, reflecting the quality and creativity of the offerings. The Hall on Franklin provides a chic, communal dining experience, complete with a full-service bar and stylish décor. When visiting these markets and food halls, it's advisable to check their official websites or social media pages for the most up-to-date information on operating hours and vendor offerings. Arriving early can help avoid crowds, especially on weekends, and allows for the best selection of goods. Embracing Tampa's market scene offers a unique and flavorful way to experience the city's local culture and culinary diversity.

6.7 Bars, Nightlife and Entertainment

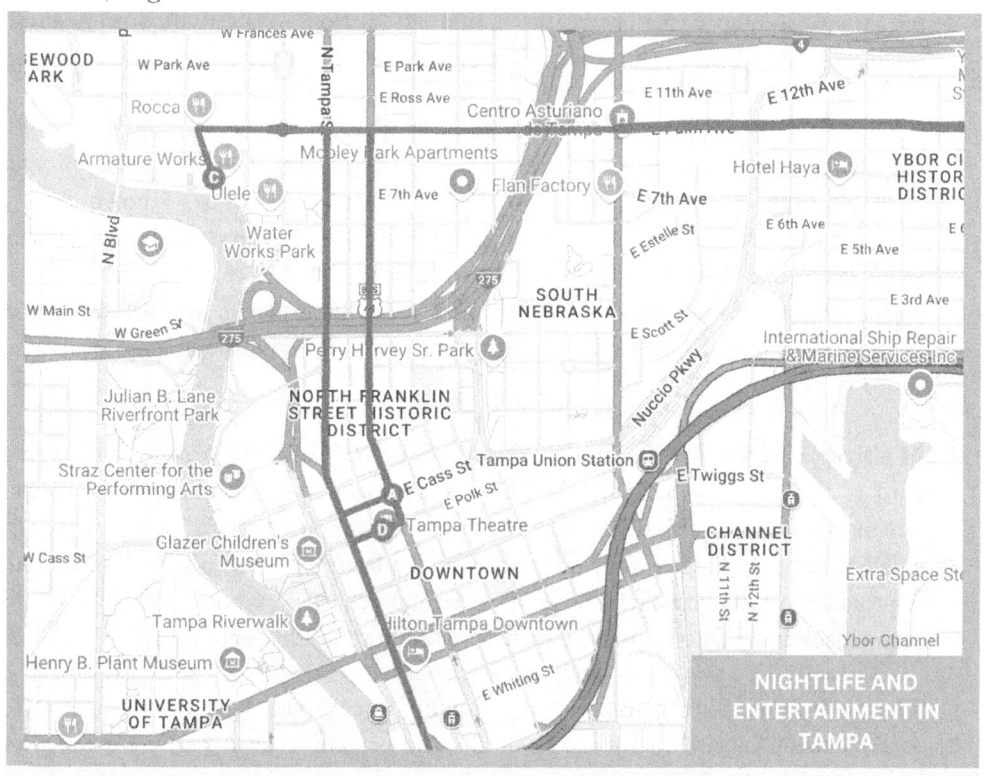

Directions from Tampa, FL, USA to The Sail Pavilion, South Franklin Street, Tampa, FL, USA

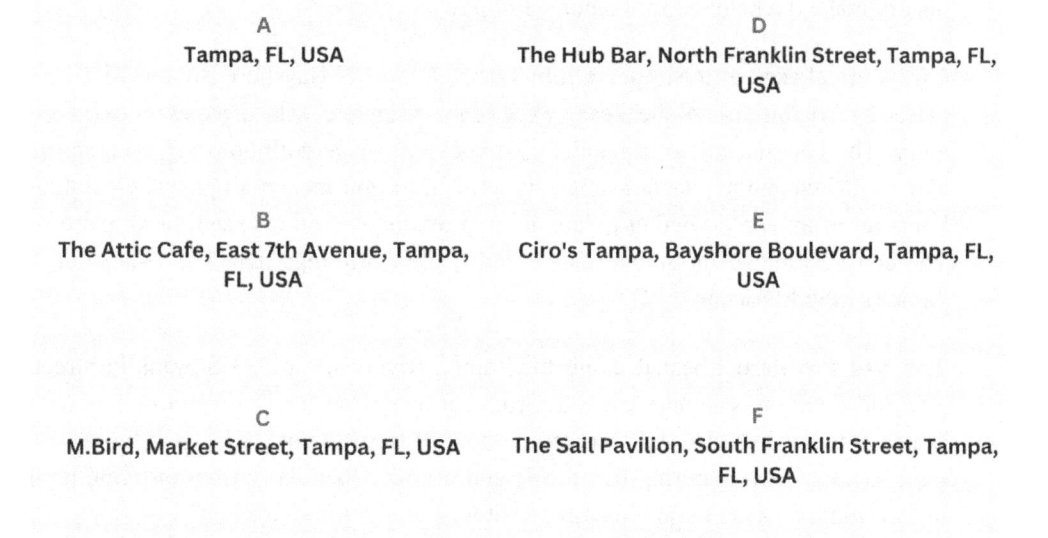

A
Tampa, FL, USA

B
The Attic Cafe, East 7th Avenue, Tampa, FL, USA

C
M.Bird, Market Street, Tampa, FL, USA

D
The Hub Bar, North Franklin Street, Tampa, FL, USA

E
Ciro's Tampa, Bayshore Boulevard, Tampa, FL, USA

F
The Sail Pavilion, South Franklin Street, Tampa, FL, USA

Tampa's nightlife offers a diverse array of bars and entertainment venues, each providing unique experiences that cater to various tastes. Exploring these establishments allows visitors to immerse themselves in the city's vibrant evening culture.

The Attic Cafe: Perched atop 500 E Kennedy Boulevard, The Attic Cafe offers a cozy atmosphere with panoramic views of downtown Tampa. Known for its selection of craft beers, wines, and specialty coffees, it also serves light fare such as sandwiches and pastries. Operating hours extend into the evening, making it a perfect spot for both daytime relaxation and nighttime gatherings. The combination of scenic vistas and a laid-back environment makes it a favorite among locals and visitors alike.

M. Bird: Located at 1903 Market Street within the Armature Works complex, M. Bird is a rooftop bar that boasts stunning views of the Hillsborough River and downtown skyline. The menu features tropical-inspired cocktails and a variety of small plates, including ceviche and sliders. Open from late afternoon until late night, it provides a chic setting for evening entertainment. The vibrant atmosphere and scenic backdrop make it a must-visit destination for nightlife enthusiasts.

The Hub Bar: Situated at 719 N Franklin Street, The Hub Bar is a historic establishment known for its strong drinks and eclectic crowd. Serving a range of classic cocktails and affordable beers, it also offers live music performances that add to its lively ambiance. Open daily from afternoon until the early morning hours, The Hub provides an authentic dive bar experience. Its unpretentious vibe and rich history make it a beloved spot among Tampa's bar-goers.

Ciro's Speakeasy and Supper Club: Located at 2109 Bayshore Boulevard, Ciro's offers a Prohibition-era speakeasy experience complete with a password-required entry. The bar specializes in handcrafted cocktails made with house-infused spirits and fresh ingredients, accompanied by a menu of gourmet small plates. Operating hours are from early evening to late night, providing an intimate setting for patrons. The combination of its unique theme and quality offerings makes it a standout in Tampa's nightlife scene.

The Sail Pavilion: Located along the Tampa Riverwalk at 333 S Franklin Street, The Sail Pavilion is an open-air waterfront bar that offers a relaxed atmosphere with scenic water views. The bar serves a variety of tropical cocktails, local beers, and light snacks, often featuring live music and events. Open daily from morning until late evening, it caters to both daytime visitors and nighttime revelers.

CHAPTER 7
DAY TRIPS AND EXCURSIONS

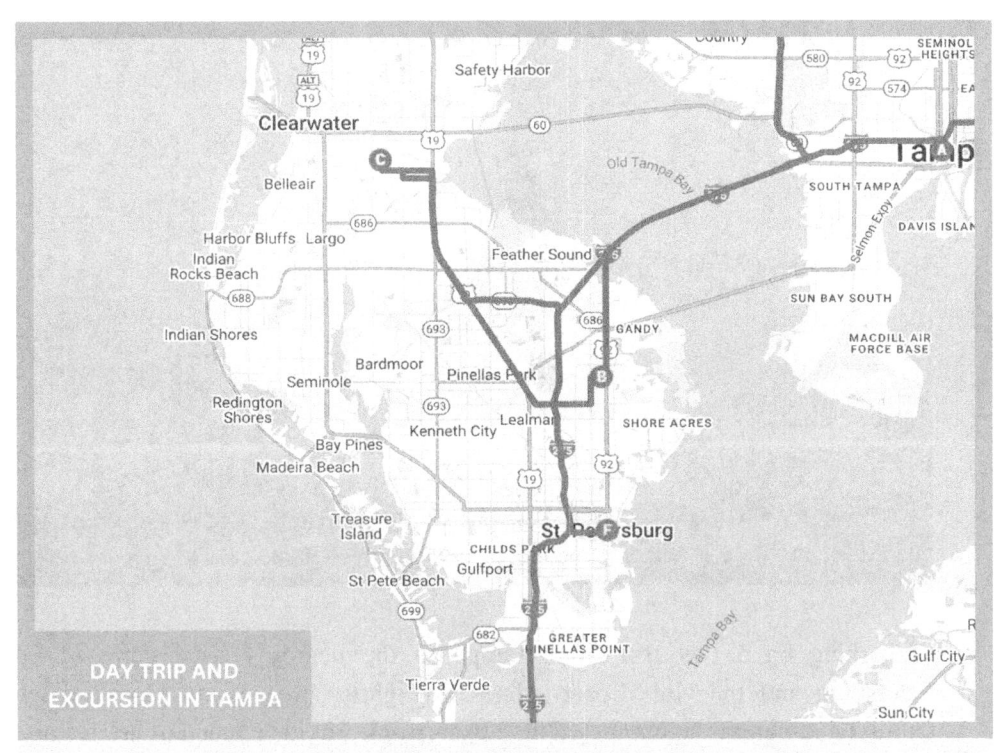

DAY TRIP AND EXCURSION IN TAMPA

Directions from Tampa, FL, USA to St. Petersburg, FL, USA

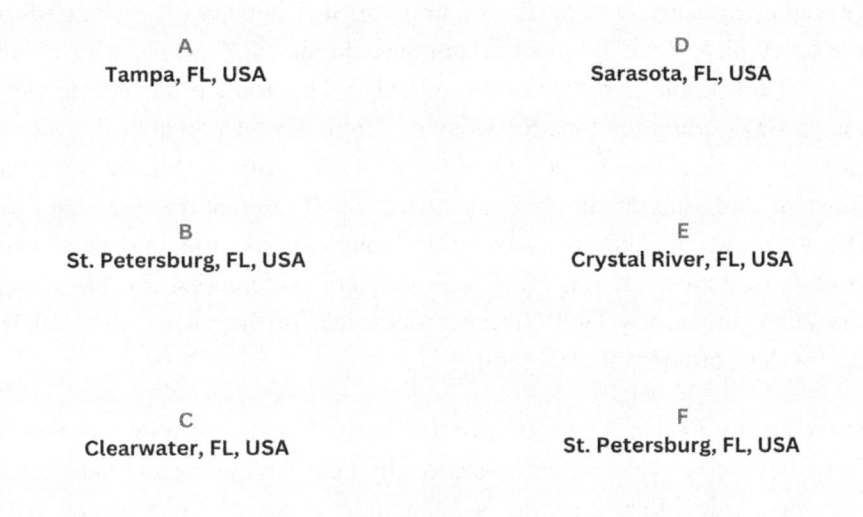

A
Tampa, FL, USA

B
St. Petersburg, FL, USA

C
Clearwater, FL, USA

D
Sarasota, FL, USA

E
Crystal River, FL, USA

F
St. Petersburg, FL, USA

7.1 St. Petersburg and the Gulf Coast

Embarking on a day trip from Tampa to the nearby coastal gems of St. Petersburg and the Gulf Coast offers a delightful escape into Florida's rich cultural and natural landscapes. These excursions provide a blend of art, history, and pristine beaches, all within a short journey from Tampa.

Traveling by Car: Driving from Tampa to St. Petersburg is a straightforward journey, typically taking about 30 minutes via the I-275 South, which includes crossing the iconic Sunshine Skyway Bridge. This route offers scenic views of Tampa Bay, setting the tone for a day of exploration. Upon arrival, visitors can immerse themselves in the vibrant arts scene, with highlights such as the Salvador Dalí Museum, housing an extensive collection of the surrealist's works. The downtown area boasts a variety of dining options, from upscale restaurants to casual eateries, catering to diverse culinary preferences. For those seeking relaxation, the nearby Gulf beaches, renowned for their soft, white sands and clear waters, provide an ideal setting.

Traveling by Ferry: An alternative and leisurely mode of transportation is the Cross-Bay Ferry, which operates seasonally between Tampa and St. Petersburg. The ferry ride offers passengers panoramic views of the bay and the city skylines, making the journey itself a memorable part of the excursion. Upon docking in St. Petersburg, visitors are within walking distance of key attractions, including the Museum of Fine Arts and the bustling St. Pete Pier, which features parks, restaurants, and shops. The ferry schedule varies, so it's advisable to check the latest timings and availability in advance.

Traveling by Bicycle: For the more adventurous, cycling from Tampa to St. Petersburg is an option, utilizing the extensive network of bike trails and lanes that connect the two cities. The Pinellas Trail, a 38-mile-long path, offers a safe and scenic route for cyclists, passing through various parks and neighborhoods. Upon reaching St. Petersburg, cyclists can explore the city's numerous bike-friendly areas, including the waterfront parks and the Grand Central District, known for its eclectic mix of shops and galleries. Bike rentals are available in both cities for those who do not have their own equipment.

Traveling by Bus: Public transportation is another viable option, with the Pinellas Suncoast Transit Authority (PSTA) offering bus services between Tampa and St. Petersburg. The journey provides an opportunity to observe the local scenery and urban landscapes. Upon arrival, visitors can explore the historic Old Northeast neighborhood, characterized by its charming brick streets and early 20th-century architecture. The nearby Sunken Gardens, a century-old botanical paradise, offers a tranquil retreat with its exotic plants and cascading waterfalls.

Traveling by Private Boat: For those with access to a private boat, traveling across Tampa Bay to the Gulf Coast is a unique and exhilarating experience. The waterways offer opportunities for fishing, dolphin watching, and enjoying the coastal vistas. Destinations such as Egmont Key State Park, accessible only by boat, provide secluded beaches and historic sites, including a 19th-century lighthouse and fort ruins. Boaters should be mindful of maritime regulations and weather conditions, ensuring a safe and enjoyable journey. Each mode of transportation to St. Petersburg and the Gulf Coast from Tampa offers its own unique experiences, catering to various preferences and interests. Whether seeking cultural enrichment, outdoor adventure, or simple relaxation, these day trips provide a rich tapestry of activities and sights that capture the essence of Florida's Gulf Coast.

7.2 Clearwater and the Beaches

Embarking on a day trip from Tampa to Clearwater and its pristine beaches offers a delightful escape into sun-soaked shores and vibrant coastal culture. Clearwater Beach, renowned for its powdery white sands and clear Gulf waters, provides an idyllic setting for relaxation and recreation.

Traveling by Car: The most convenient way to reach Clearwater from Tampa is by car. A scenic drive of approximately 25 miles westward via State Road 60 leads directly to the heart of Clearwater Beach. This route, known as the Courtney Campbell Causeway, offers travelers picturesque views of Tampa Bay, enhancing the journey. Upon arrival, ample parking facilities are available near the beach, though it's advisable to arrive early during peak seasons to secure a spot.

Public Transportation Options: For those preferring public transit, the Pinellas Suncoast Transit Authority (PSTA) operates the Clearwater Jolley Trolley, which connects downtown Clearwater with the beach area. Travelers can take a bus from Tampa to downtown Clearwater and then transfer to the Jolley Trolley for a charming ride to the beach. This option provides a leisurely pace, allowing visitors to enjoy the local scenery without the concerns of driving and parking.

Cycling Adventures: For the more adventurous, cycling from Tampa to Clearwater is feasible via the Courtney Campbell Trail, a dedicated bike path running parallel to the causeway. Spanning about 9.5 miles, this trail offers cyclists stunning waterfront vistas and designated rest areas. Upon reaching

Clearwater, numerous bike racks are available, making it convenient to secure bicycles while exploring the beach and nearby attractions.

Exploring Clearwater Beach: Once in Clearwater, visitors are greeted by the iconic Pier 60, a hub of activity featuring local artisans, street performers, and breathtaking sunsets celebrated nightly. The beach's soft, white sands and gentle Gulf waves make it ideal for sunbathing, swimming, and water sports. The nearby Clearwater Marine Aquarium offers insights into marine life conservation and is home to Winter, the famous dolphin with a prosthetic tail.

Cultural and Historical Significance: Clearwater's history is rich with indigenous heritage and development as a coastal retreat. The city's evolution from a modest settlement to a bustling tourist destination reflects its enduring appeal. Visitors can explore local museums and historical sites to gain a deeper appreciation of the area's past and its cultural tapestry. A day trip to Clearwater from Tampa promises a harmonious blend of relaxation, adventure, and cultural enrichment, making it a must-visit destination for those seeking to experience Florida's coastal charm.

7.3 Sarasota and the Cultural Coast

Embarking on a day trip from Tampa to Sarasota and Florida's Cultural Coast offers a rich tapestry of experiences, blending artistic heritage with natural beauty. This journey unveils a region celebrated for its vibrant arts scene, pristine beaches, and historical landmarks.

Traveling by Car: The most convenient way to reach Sarasota from Tampa is by car, a journey of approximately 60 miles south via Interstate 75, typically taking around an hour. This route provides a smooth drive, leading travelers directly into the heart of Sarasota. Upon arrival, the John and Mable Ringling Museum of Art stands as a testament to the city's cultural richness, housing an extensive collection of European paintings and a fascinating circus museum. The museum's lush gardens and the historic Ca' d'Zan mansion offer glimpses into the opulent past of the Ringling family. Visitors can explore the museum's diverse exhibits, stroll through the meticulously maintained gardens, and admire the Venetian Gothic architecture of the mansion.

Traveling by Bus: For those preferring public transportation, bus services operate between Tampa and Sarasota, though they may require transfers and longer travel times. Upon reaching Sarasota, the Marie Selby Botanical Gardens await, renowned for their collection of epiphytic plants, including orchids and bromeliads. The gardens provide a tranquil escape, with pathways meandering through tropical displays and bayfront sanctuaries. Visitors can immerse themselves in the vibrant flora, explore the on-site research facilities, and enjoy panoramic views of Sarasota Bay.

Traveling by Train: While there is no direct train service between Tampa and Sarasota, travelers can consider combining train and bus routes, though this requires careful planning and may extend travel time. Once in Sarasota, the historic downtown area beckons with its charming boutiques, art galleries, and theaters. The Sarasota Opera House, a beautifully restored 1920s venue, offers performances that reflect the city's artistic spirit. Strolling through the downtown streets, visitors can appreciate the blend of historic architecture and modern cultural offerings.

Traveling by Boat: For a unique approach, private boat charters can navigate the Intracoastal Waterway from Tampa to Sarasota, offering scenic views of Florida's coastline. Upon docking, Siesta Key Beach awaits with its powdery white sands and clear turquoise waters, consistently ranked among the top beaches in the United States. The beach's quartz-crystal sand remains cool underfoot, providing a perfect setting for sunbathing, swimming, or simply enjoying the coastal ambiance. Nearby, the Siesta Key Village offers a variety of dining and shopping options, enhancing the beachside experience.

Traveling by Air: While air travel between Tampa and Sarasota is uncommon due to the short distance, private flights are an option for those seeking expedited travel. Upon arrival, the Mote Marine Laboratory & Aquarium offers insights into marine research and conservation. Exhibits feature a diverse array of sea life, including manatees, sea turtles, and sharks. Interactive displays and educational programs provide an engaging experience for visitors of all ages, highlighting the importance of marine ecosystems. Each mode of transportation to Sarasota and the Cultural Coast from Tampa presents its own unique experiences, catering to various preferences and interests. Whether drawn by the allure of world-class museums, the serenity of botanical gardens, or the charm of historic districts, visitors will find Sarasota a destination rich in cultural and natural treasures.

7.4 Crystal River and the Nature Coast

Embarking on a day trip from Tampa to Crystal River and Florida's Nature Coast offers an immersive experience into the state's pristine natural beauty and rich wildlife. Located approximately 90 miles north of Tampa, Crystal River is renowned for its clear springs and as a habitat for the gentle West Indian manatee.

Traveling by Car: The most straightforward way to reach Crystal River is by car. A drive of about 1.5 to 2 hours via the Suncoast Parkway (State Road 589) leads directly to this charming coastal town. The route is scenic, with glimpses of Florida's diverse landscapes, making the journey as enjoyable as the destination. Upon arrival, ample parking is available near major attractions, facilitating easy exploration.

Public Transportation Options: For those preferring public transit, options are limited due to the region's rural nature. However, regional bus services connect

Tampa to nearby cities, from which local transportation can be arranged to reach Crystal River. It's advisable to plan ahead and check current schedules to ensure a smooth journey.

Guided Tours and Shuttles: Several tour operators in Tampa offer day trips to Crystal River, including transportation. These guided excursions often feature activities such as swimming with manatees, kayaking, or exploring the area's natural springs. Opting for a tour provides the convenience of organized travel and the expertise of local guides.

Exploring Crystal River and the Nature Coast; Upon reaching Crystal River, visitors are greeted by the allure of Three Sisters Springs, a sanctuary known for its crystal-clear waters and as a winter refuge for manatees. The springs' ethereal beauty, with sunlight filtering through turquoise waters surrounded by lush vegetation, offers a serene setting for kayaking, snorkeling, or simply observing wildlife. The cultural significance of Crystal River is highlighted by the Crystal River Archaeological State Park, where ancient Native American mounds and artifacts provide insight into the region's early inhabitants. Exploring these historical sites offers a glimpse into the area's rich past and its longstanding connection to the natural environment. The broader Nature Coast region encompasses a stretch of Florida's Gulf Coast celebrated for its unspoiled landscapes, diverse ecosystems, and outdoor recreational opportunities. Activities such as birdwatching, hiking, and fishing are popular, with numerous parks and preserves offering well-maintained trails and facilities. A day trip to Crystal River and the Nature Coast from Tampa provides a harmonious blend of adventure, relaxation, and education, allowing visitors to experience Florida's natural splendors and cultural heritage in a single, enriching excursion.

7.5 Exploring Tampa's Neighboring Cities

Venturing beyond Tampa reveals a tapestry of neighboring cities, each offering unique cultural, historical, and natural attractions. These nearby destinations provide enriching experiences that complement the vibrant life of Tampa.

St. Petersburg: Located just across the bay from Tampa, St. Petersburg is renowned for its vibrant arts scene and beautiful waterfront parks. The city is home to the Salvador Dalí Museum, which houses an extensive collection of the surrealist artist's works. Visitors can also explore the revitalized St. Pete Pier, offering dining, shopping, and panoramic views of Tampa Bay. The city's downtown area boasts a variety of galleries, boutiques, and cafes, reflecting its creative spirit.

Clearwater: Situated to the west of Tampa, Clearwater is famed for its pristine beaches and clear Gulf waters. Clearwater Beach consistently ranks among the top beaches in the United States, attracting visitors with its soft white sands and vibrant atmosphere. The nearby Clearwater Marine Aquarium is dedicated to the rescue and rehabilitation of marine animals, offering educational exhibits and the chance to see rescued dolphins and sea turtles up close. The city's lively Pier 60 hosts nightly festivals featuring local artisans and street performers, making it a hub of activity, especially during sunset.

Sarasota: South of Tampa lies Sarasota, a city celebrated for its cultural institutions and stunning coastal landscapes. The John and Mable Ringling Museum of Art showcases an impressive collection of European paintings, while the adjacent Ca' d'Zan mansion reflects the opulence of the Roaring Twenties. Nature enthusiasts can visit the Marie Selby Botanical Gardens, renowned for its collection of orchids and tropical plants. Sarasota's Siesta Key Beach is famous for its quartz-crystal sand, offering a serene setting for relaxation.

Lakeland: To the east of Tampa, Lakeland is known for its numerous lakes and historic charm. The city's downtown area features well-preserved early 20th-century architecture, housing a variety of shops, restaurants, and cultural venues. The Polk Museum of Art offers diverse exhibitions, while the annual Sun 'n Fun Aerospace Expo attracts aviation enthusiasts from around the world. Visitors can also explore the extensive collection of Frank Lloyd Wright architecture at Florida Southern College, the largest single-site collection of his work.

Bradenton: Southwest of Tampa, Bradenton offers a blend of cultural attractions and natural beauty. The Village of the Arts, a vibrant community of artists, features colorful cottages housing galleries, studios, and cafes. The South Florida Museum provides insights into the region's history and marine life, including a planetarium and the beloved manatee, Snooty. Bradenton's Riverwalk, a 1.5-mile park along the Manatee River, offers scenic views, playgrounds, and an amphitheater for live performances.

Tarpon Springs: Northwest of Tampa, Tarpon Springs is known for its rich Greek heritage and historic sponge docks. Visitors can explore the Sponge Docks District, where shops offer natural sponges, handmade soaps, and Mediterranean imports. Authentic Greek restaurants line the streets, serving traditional dishes like moussaka and baklava. The city's Epiphany celebration, held annually in January, is one of the largest in the Western Hemisphere, reflecting its deep-rooted cultural traditions. Each of these neighboring cities offers a distinct experience, enriching any visit to the Tampa Bay area with their unique attractions and cultural offerings.

CHAPTER 8
EVENTS AND FESTIVALS

8.1 Gasparilla Pirate Festival

Tampa's Gasparilla Pirate Festival is an iconic annual event that transforms the city into a vibrant, swashbuckling spectacle. Taking place each January, this legendary festival brings together thousands of visitors and locals for a celebration inspired by the infamous pirate José Gaspar. Known simply as "Gasparilla," this festival is a blend of history, revelry, and community spirit, making it one of the most anticipated events in Florida. From the grand pirate invasion to the electrifying parade, this is a must-attend festival for those seeking adventure, entertainment, and a deep dive into Tampa's cultural heritage.

Location and How to Get There: Gasparilla takes place along Tampa's scenic Bayshore Boulevard, offering a waterfront backdrop to the festivities. The event kicks off near the Tampa Convention Center, where the famous pirate invasion occurs before leading into the lively Parade of Pirates. Visitors traveling to Gasparilla can arrive by car, though parking can be limited due to the massive crowds. Ride-sharing services like Uber and Lyft are popular options, as well as public transportation, including the TECO Line Streetcar. Some attendees even arrive by boat, docking at nearby marinas to experience the excitement from the water.

The Pirate Invasion and Parade of Pirates: At the heart of Gasparilla is the thrilling pirate invasion, an event that pays homage to the mythical José Gaspar and his band of buccaneers. A massive pirate ship, the José Gasparilla, sails into Tampa Bay, "invading" the city with a flotilla of boats trailing behind. Once they reach shore, the pirates take over the city in dramatic fashion, marching through the streets in full pirate regalia. Following the invasion, the Parade of Pirates takes center stage, featuring elaborate floats, marching bands, and costumed revelers tossing beads to the cheering crowds. This parade is one of the largest in the United States, attracting hundreds of thousands of spectators each year.

Cultural and Historical Significance: Gasparilla is more than just a lively festival; it is deeply rooted in Tampa's history and cultural identity. Established in 1904, the festival was created to celebrate the legendary pirate José Gaspar, who, according to local folklore, terrorized Florida's Gulf Coast. While the legend itself is shrouded in mystery, the festival has grown into a beloved tradition that reflects the city's spirit of camaraderie and fun. Over the decades, Gasparilla has evolved into a multifaceted celebration, incorporating music, art, and family-friendly activities while maintaining its signature pirate theme.

What to Do at Gasparilla: Gasparilla offers a variety of experiences beyond the invasion and parade, ensuring that visitors of all ages find something to enjoy. For families, the Gasparilla Children's Parade provides a kid-friendly alternative with a focus on safety and entertainment. Live music performances take place throughout the city, featuring local and national artists. Food vendors serve up Tampa's best flavors, from Cuban sandwiches to fresh seafood. The Gasparilla Art Festival showcases works from talented artists, adding a creative dimension to the event. Visitors can also explore the Gasparilla Outbound Voyage, where the pirates "surrender" the city in a final celebration before setting sail once again.

Entry Fees and Viewing Options: Gasparilla is a free public event, with ample space along the parade route for attendees to enjoy the festivities. However, those looking for a more exclusive experience can purchase reserved seating along Bayshore Boulevard. VIP areas offer premium views, private seating, and additional amenities such as food and beverage options. For those who prefer to watch from the water, boat charters provide front-row seats to the pirate invasion. Regardless of how you experience Gasparilla, arriving early is key to securing the best spot.

Tips for Visitors and What to Expect: To fully enjoy Gasparilla, it's essential to come prepared. Wearing pirate-themed attire is highly encouraged, as it adds to the excitement and allows attendees to immerse themselves in the spirit of the festival. Comfortable shoes are a must, as the event requires a lot of walking. Since Tampa's weather in January can be unpredictable, it's a good idea to dress in layers. Visitors should also bring cash for food vendors and souvenir purchases, as some stalls may not accept cards. Most importantly, it's crucial to plan ahead for transportation, as road closures and heavy traffic are common during the event.

Why Gasparilla is Worth Visiting: Gasparilla is more than just a parade; it is an experience that captures the essence of Tampa's lively and welcoming atmosphere. The festival's blend of history, community pride, and festive spirit makes it a one-of-a-kind event that draws visitors from around the country. Whether you're a first-time attendee or a returning guest, Gasparilla offers new surprises and unforgettable moments with every visit. From the exhilarating pirate invasion to the high-energy street celebrations, Gasparilla is a must-see festival that showcases Tampa's unique culture in a spectacular fashion.

8.2 Tampa Bay Blues Festival

Every April, the city of St. Petersburg, Florida, comes alive with the soulful sounds of the Tampa Bay Blues Festival. Held at the picturesque Vinoy Waterfront Park, this renowned event has been a staple in the blues community since its inception in 1995. The festival spans three days, typically in mid-April, attracting music enthusiasts from around the globe. In 2025, the festival is scheduled for April 11th through 13th, promising another unforgettable experience.

A Stunning Venue at Vinoy Waterfront Park; Vinoy Waterfront Park, located at 701 Bayshore Drive N.E., St. Petersburg, offers a breathtaking backdrop for the festival, with expansive green spaces and sweeping views of Tampa Bay. Attendees can enjoy performances from both legendary blues artists and emerging talents, creating a diverse and dynamic lineup. The festival's atmosphere is electric, with music complemented by a variety of food vendors, full-service bars, and arts and crafts stalls, ensuring there is something for everyone. This setting enhances the experience, allowing visitors to immerse themselves in the rhythm of the blues while enjoying the beauty of Florida's Gulf Coast.

How to Get to the Festival: Reaching the Tampa Bay Blues Festival is convenient, whether you are a local or traveling from afar. St. Petersburg is accessible via major highways, and ample parking is available near the venue. Many attendees opt for ride-sharing services to avoid parking hassles, and for those preferring public transportation, local transit services provide routes that stop close to the park. Some visitors choose to stay in nearby hotels, many of which offer shuttle services to the festival grounds. Given the festival's popularity, it is advisable to plan your journey in advance to ensure a smooth arrival.

Tickets and Entry Fees: Tickets for the Tampa Bay Blues Festival can be purchased in advance through the official website. Options range from single-day general admission passes to three-day VIP packages, catering to various preferences and budgets. VIP passes offer perks such as front-stage seating, complimentary food and beverages, and access to exclusive areas, enhancing the festival experience. Prices vary depending on the ticket type and purchase date, so early booking is recommended to secure the best rates. General admission tickets typically start at $50 per day, while VIP passes can range from $300 to $600 for the entire weekend.

The Cultural and Historical Significance of the Festival: Attending the Tampa Bay Blues Festival is more than just a musical experience; it is a cultural immersion into the heart of blues music. The festival has a rich history of showcasing top-tier blues talent, contributing significantly to the preservation and celebration of this iconic genre. Beyond the music, the event fosters a sense of community, bringing together people from diverse backgrounds to share in the joy of live performances. The festival also supports local charities, with proceeds benefiting organizations such as PARC, which assists individuals with developmental disabilities. Over the years, the festival has helped keep blues music alive, honoring both legendary and up-and-coming artists who continue to shape the genre.

Things to Do at the Festival: Beyond the exhilarating performances, the Tampa Bay Blues Festival offers an array of activities for visitors. Food lovers can indulge in a variety of cuisines, from Southern barbecue to fresh seafood, with vendors serving up authentic flavors that complement the music. The festival's artisan market features handcrafted goods, artwork, and unique souvenirs, giving attendees a chance to take a piece of the experience home. For those who want a break from the music, VIP lounges and shaded rest areas provide a place to unwind. The festival's setting near downtown St. Petersburg also allows visitors to explore local attractions, including galleries, waterfront parks, and historical landmarks.

Exploring St. Petersburg After the Festival: For visitors, the festival offers a chance to explore the vibrant city of St. Petersburg. The downtown area, with its array of restaurants, shops, and cultural attractions, is within walking distance of the park. The nearby Salvador Dalí Museum and the Museum of Fine Arts provide enriching experiences for art enthusiasts. Additionally, St. Pete Beach and the Sunken Gardens are just a short drive away, offering a perfect opportunity to relax before or after the festival. Whether it's dining at waterfront restaurants, strolling through historic neighborhoods, or taking in the stunning views of Tampa Bay, St. Petersburg has plenty to offer festival goers looking to extend their trip.

Why You Should Attend the Tampa Bay Blues Festival: The Tampa Bay Blues Festival is a must-visit event for music lovers and cultural enthusiasts alike. Its blend of world-class performances, scenic location, and community spirit makes it a standout occasion in Florida's event calendar. Whether you are drawn by the soulful melodies, the vibrant atmosphere, or the chance to be part of a longstanding tradition, this festival promises an experience that will resonate long after the final note has been played. The combination of incredible music, delicious food, and stunning waterfront views makes this festival an unforgettable getaway for those looking to experience the best of Tampa Bay's cultural scene.

8.3 Florida Strawberry Festival

The Florida Strawberry Festival is an annual event held in Plant City, Florida, known for its rich agricultural heritage and world-renowned strawberries. Each year, from late February to early March, this festival brings together locals and visitors for a celebration of fresh produce, live entertainment, and family-friendly attractions. The festival is a tribute to the hardworking farmers who cultivate the region's prized strawberries, making it one of the most anticipated events in the state. In 2025, the festival will take place from February 27 to March 9, offering a mix of tradition, fun, and delicious strawberry-themed treats.

Location and How to Get There: The Florida Strawberry Festival is hosted at 303 BerryFest Place in Plant City, located just east of Tampa. Travelers can reach the festival by car via Interstate 4, taking Exit 21 at Forbes Road and following signs to the venue. Parking is available on-site, with various lots offering easy access to the festival grounds. Public transportation options are limited, but ride-sharing services such as Uber and Lyft provide convenient alternatives for those traveling from nearby cities. The journey from Tampa to Plant City takes approximately 30 minutes, making it a quick and enjoyable day trip.

Entry Fees and Ticket Information: The Florida Strawberry Festival offers reasonably priced admission, making it accessible for families and individuals alike. Tickets can be purchased online in advance or at the entrance on the day of the event. Special discounted tickets are often available at select Publix supermarkets across Central Florida prior to the festival. While general admission covers access to the festival grounds and most attractions, additional fees may apply for certain rides, concerts, and premium experiences. Visitors should check the festival's official website for up-to-date pricing and special promotions.

Why the Festival is Worth Visiting: Attending the Florida Strawberry Festival provides a unique opportunity to experience the agricultural traditions and hospitality of Plant City. With its reputation as the "Winter Strawberry Capital of the World," Plant City yields a staggering quantity of strawberries every year. . Visitors can indulge in freshly picked strawberries, homemade strawberry shortcake, and an assortment of strawberry-themed desserts. Beyond the food, the festival showcases the region's rich history and community pride, making it an authentic and unforgettable experience.

The History and Cultural Significance of the Festival: The Florida Strawberry Festival dates back to 1930 when local farmers and civic leaders sought to celebrate the annual strawberry harvest. Over the decades, the festival has grown into a large-scale event featuring concerts, parades, and competitions. The festival honors Plant City's agricultural roots while incorporating modern attractions that appeal to visitors of all ages. It remains a symbol of Florida's farming heritage, bringing generations together to celebrate the region's most beloved crop.

What to Do at the Florida Strawberry Festival: Visitors to the Florida Strawberry Festival can enjoy a wide variety of activities and entertainment. Live music performances take place throughout the festival, featuring both nationally recognized artists and local talent. The festival's midway boasts carnival rides, games, and interactive attractions for families. Agricultural exhibits highlight the importance of farming in Florida, with opportunities to learn about the strawberry-growing process and even participate in hands-on activities. Beauty pageants, eating contests, and craft fairs add to the festive atmosphere, ensuring there is something for everyone to enjoy.

Tips for Making the Most of Your Visit: To fully enjoy the Florida Strawberry Festival, visitors should plan their trip in advance. Arriving early is recommended to avoid long lines and secure parking close to the entrance. Comfortable clothing and footwear are essential for navigating the festival grounds, which can get crowded during peak hours. Bringing cash is advised, as some food vendors and smaller attractions may not accept credit cards. Checking the festival schedule ahead of time allows visitors to plan their day around performances, contests, and other special events.

Why You Shouldn't Miss the Florida Strawberry Festival: The Florida Strawberry Festival is more than just a fair—it's a celebration of agriculture, community, and tradition. Whether you come for the delicious strawberries, exciting entertainment, or family-friendly atmosphere, the festival offers a memorable experience that captures the essence of Florida's farming culture. With its rich history, vibrant energy, and mouthwatering treats, the Florida Strawberry Festival is a must-visit event for anyone looking to experience the heart and soul of Plant City.

8.4 Tampa Bay Margarita Festival

Each year, as the warmth of late May envelops Tampa, the city comes alive with the vibrant energy of the Tampa Bay Margarita Festival. This eagerly anticipated event, often referred to by locals as the "Margarita Fest," is traditionally held over Memorial Day weekend, offering attendees a perfect blend of refreshing beverages, live music, and a festive atmosphere. It has become one of the most celebrated summer events in the region, drawing thousands of visitors who come to indulge in craft margaritas and soak in the lively atmosphere.

A Stunning Venue at Julian B. Lane Riverfront Park: The festival takes place at the scenic Julian B. Lane Riverfront Park, located at 1001 North Boulevard, Tampa, FL. This stunning waterfront park provides a picturesque backdrop, with expansive green spaces, scenic river views, and plenty of open-air seating for festivalgoers. The park's layout allows for a smooth flow of crowds, ensuring that attendees can easily move between the different margarita stations, food vendors, and entertainment areas. The combination of nature and vibrant festival energy makes it one of the best locations for an outdoor event in Tampa.

How to Get to the Festival: Reaching Tampa Bay Margarita Festival is convenient whether you're driving, using public transportation, or opting for a ride-share service. The venue is easily accessible via I-275, and parking options are available at nearby garages and lots. For those relying on public transit, HART buses and the Tampa Streetcar provide routes that stop near the festival grounds. Many visitors choose ride-sharing services like Uber and Lyft to avoid the hassle of parking. Given the popularity of the event, early arrival is recommended to secure the best spots and enjoy the festival without long wait times.

Entry Fee and Ticket Options; Attending the Tampa Bay Margarita Festival requires a ticket purchase, with various options to suit different preferences. General admission tickets grant access to the main event areas, allowing attendees to explore multiple margarita stations, food vendors, and live music performances. VIP packages offer additional perks such as exclusive seating, premium margarita selections, and private restrooms. Ticket prices typically range from $35 to $200, depending on the package and purchase date. Early bird discounts are available for those who book in advance, making it a great idea to secure tickets ahead of time.

The Cultural and Historical Significance of the Festival: The Tampa Bay Margarita Festival is more than just an event; it's a cultural celebration that embodies the spirit of Tampa's diverse community. Margaritas, originating from Mexico, have long been associated with celebration, relaxation, and good times. The festival embraces this tradition, creating an immersive experience where visitors can taste a variety of handcrafted margaritas, from classic lime to bold and tropical infusions. The event has grown over the years to become one of the biggest margarita festivals in Florida, drawing visitors from across the country.

Live Music and Entertainment; One of the biggest draws of the Tampa Bay Margarita Festival is its impressive lineup of live music performances. The festival features a mix of local bands, national headliners, and legendary rock, country, and reggae artists, ensuring a diverse soundtrack for the day. The music blends perfectly with the festive atmosphere, encouraging visitors to dance, relax on the lawn, and sing along to their favorite hits. The night ends with a spectacular fireworks show, lighting up the sky above Tampa Bay, making for a perfect festival finale.

The Ultimate Margarita Experience; Margaritas take center stage at this festival, with dozens of vendors offering unique twists on the classic cocktail. Visitors can expect everything from traditional lime margaritas to creative flavors like spicy jalapeño, mango habanero, coconut, and passionfruit. Craft margarita bars showcase premium tequila brands, while frozen margarita machines keep guests cool in the Florida heat. Festivalgoers also have the option to attend tequila tastings, where experts guide them through the nuances of different varieties and cocktail pairings.

Food Vendors and Local Cuisine: No festival experience is complete without delicious food, and the Tampa Bay Margarita Festival delivers with an array of food trucks and local vendors serving up mouthwatering dishes. Attendees can enjoy a variety of Tex-Mex specialties, gourmet tacos, barbecue, fresh seafood, and Latin-inspired snacks. Many of the dishes are designed to pair perfectly with margaritas, offering a bold and flavorful dining experience. Vegetarian and vegan options are also available, ensuring that everyone can find something to enjoy.

Things to Do Beyond the Drinks: While margaritas and live music take center stage, there are plenty of other activities and attractions to explore at the festival. Interactive games, giveaways, and photo booths provide entertainment throughout the day, allowing visitors to engage in fun challenges and take home memorable souvenirs. Many festivalgoers enjoy lounging by the waterfront, soaking up the sun, and taking in the breathtaking views of Tampa Bay. The laid-back yet energetic atmosphere makes this festival a must-visit event for both locals and tourists.

Why You Should Attend the Tampa Bay Margarita Festival: The Tampa Bay Margarita Festival is a celebration of great drinks, music, and community spirit, making it one of the most exciting events in the region. Whether you are a margarita enthusiast, a music lover, or someone looking for a fun weekend escape, this festival delivers an unforgettable experience. The combination of craft cocktails, vibrant entertainment, and the stunning waterfront setting makes it a must-attend event for anyone visiting Tampa in late May. From handcrafted margaritas to lively performances and mouthwatering food, the festival offers something for everyone, ensuring that attendees leave with lasting memories.

8.5 Outback Bowl and College Football

The ReliaQuest Bowl, formerly known as the Outback Bowl, is one of Tampa's most highly anticipated annual sporting events. Taking place on New Year's Eve or New Year's Day, this college football showdown features teams from the Southeastern Conference (SEC) and the Big Ten Conference. Football fans from across the country flock to Raymond James Stadium to witness some of the best collegiate talent compete for postseason glory. The atmosphere is electric, filled with passionate fans, exciting pre-game festivities, and Tampa's signature hospitality.

Location and How to Get There: The game is hosted at Raymond James Stadium, located at 4201 North Dale Mabry Highway, a central location within Tampa. Visitors arriving from out of town can easily access the stadium via major highways, including I-275 and I-4. For those relying on public transportation, Tampa's bus services offer routes that stop near the stadium. Ride-sharing services like Uber and Lyft also provide convenient drop-off and pick-up points near the venue. With thousands of fans attending, arriving early is recommended to secure parking and enjoy the full game-day experience.

Entry Fees and Ticket Information: Tickets for the ReliaQuest Bowl can be purchased online through Ticketmaster and the official bowl website. Prices vary depending on seat location, with general admission tickets starting at around $80, while premium club seats can go up to $170. Fans who wish to enhance their experience can opt for VIP seating, which offers better views and exclusive amenities. Group ticket discounts are often available for larger parties, making the game accessible for families and friends looking to attend together. With demand being high, securing tickets early ensures the best seating options and pricing.

Why the ReliaQuest Bowl is Worth Visiting: Attending the ReliaQuest Bowl is about more than just watching a football game—it's a full-fledged event that showcases Tampa's passion for sports and entertainment. The excitement begins well before kickoff with a week-long series of festivities, including team pep rallies, fan tailgates, and interactive experiences. The game itself is a thrilling competition featuring powerhouse college teams, creating an unforgettable experience for both dedicated football enthusiasts and casual fans. Beyond the stadium, Tampa's warm weather and vibrant atmosphere make it the perfect place to celebrate the New Year with fellow sports lovers.

The History and Cultural Significance of the Bowl: The ReliaQuest Bowl has been a part of Tampa's rich sports history since its inception in 1986. Originally named the Hall of Fame Bowl before becoming the Outback Bowl in 1995, the event has consistently drawn top-tier college football programs. Over the years, it has grown into a prestigious postseason matchup that garners national attention. The game not only brings excitement to Tampa but also provides a significant economic boost to the local community. For football players and fans alike, competing or attending this event is a tradition that carries historical weight and cultural significance.

What to Do at the ReliaQuest Bowl: Fans attending the ReliaQuest Bowl can expect an action-packed day filled with entertainment both on and off the field. Tailgating is a major part of the game-day experience, with fans arriving early to fire up the grill, play games, and celebrate their teams. The pre-game festivities include marching band performances, cheer squads, and live music, creating a high-energy atmosphere. Inside the stadium, visitors can enjoy a variety of food and beverage options, from classic stadium fare to local Tampa cuisine. After the game, the celebration continues at Tampa's numerous bars, restaurants, and entertainment districts.

Tips for Making the Most of Your Visit: To fully enjoy the ReliaQuest Bowl, planning ahead is essential. Arriving early ensures a smoother parking experience and allows fans to soak in the pre-game activities. Wearing team colors and bringing essential items like sunscreen and sunglasses is recommended, as Tampa's weather can be warm even in winter. Since food and drinks inside the stadium can be pricey, visitors may want to grab a meal at one of Tampa's nearby restaurants before heading in. Checking the official bowl website for event updates, stadium policies, and recommended accommodations will help make the trip even more enjoyable.

Why You Shouldn't Miss the ReliaQuest Bowl: The ReliaQuest Bowl is an iconic event that brings together college football's best teams, passionate fans, and the excitement of Tampa's dynamic atmosphere. Whether you're a devoted supporter of a competing school or simply looking for an unforgettable sports experience, this bowl game delivers in every way. The combination of high-level competition, thrilling entertainment, and Tampa's welcoming hospitality makes the ReliaQuest Bowl a must-attend event. There's no better way to kick off the new year than by experiencing the electric energy of college football in one of Florida's most exciting cities.

CONCLUSION AND RECOMMENDATIONS

Tampa is more than just a city—it is an experience, a vibrant destination where history, culture, adventure, and relaxation blend seamlessly under the warmth of the Florida sun. From its bustling waterfront districts to its pristine beaches, from its world-class dining to its rich historical sites, Tampa offers something special for every traveler. Whether you are a first-time visitor or someone returning to rediscover its magic, this city continues to surprise and captivate. The pages of this Tampa Comprehensive Travel Guide 2025 have unfolded the very essence of this beautiful city, offering insights that will transform an ordinary trip into an extraordinary one. As you stand on the threshold of planning your visit, imagine the thrill of walking along the Tampa Riverwalk, feeling the gentle breeze as the city lights dance on the water. Picture yourself savoring the freshest seafood at a waterside restaurant in Ybor City, where every bite tells a story of cultural fusion. Envision the rush of excitement as you plunge down the thrilling rides at Busch Gardens or take in the serenity of Fort De Soto Park's unspoiled beaches. This is the Tampa experience—a symphony of adventure and tranquility, history and modernity, excitement and relaxation.

Tampa is not just a place to visit; it is a place to immerse yourself in. The city invites travelers to delve into its rich heritage, whether through the Cuban cigars and historic streets of Ybor City or the world-class art collections at the Tampa Museum of Art. Nature lovers will find endless beauty, from the crystal-clear waters of its Gulf Coast beaches to the lush greenery of its many parks and gardens. Tampa is also a playground for thrill-seekers, offering everything from roller coasters to wildlife encounters, kayaking to skydiving, and sporting events to live music festivals. But what truly makes Tampa unforgettable is its spirit—a warm, welcoming energy that makes every traveler feel at home. It is the laughter of people gathered at Sparkman Wharf, the sound of waves crashing at Clearwater Beach, the aroma of fresh coffee drifting from a local café in Hyde Park. It is the community, the people, the culture, and the unmistakable vibrancy that fills the air. To truly embrace Tampa, take the time to explore beyond the well-known attractions. Discover the hidden gems—the cozy jazz bars, the independent art galleries, and the lesser-known nature trails where you can escape the crowds. Wake up early to watch the sunrise over the bay, then spend your day indulging in everything this city has to offer. Try something new, whether it is tasting an unfamiliar dish, paddleboarding for the first time, or taking part in a local festival.

Plan ahead but leave room for spontaneity. Tampa is a city best experienced with an open mind and a curious heart. Wander through its streets, strike up conversations with locals, and let yourself be swept up in its energy. Whether you are seeking adventure, relaxation, history, or entertainment, Tampa offers an itinerary that is as diverse and dynamic as the travelers who visit. For those who cherish history, dive deep into the city's Cuban, Spanish, and indigenous roots by exploring museums, historic landmarks, and cultural centers. If food is your passion, embark on a culinary adventure through Tampa's diverse restaurants, from high-end fine dining to charming local eateries. If you are a beach lover, spend your days soaking up the Florida sun on Tampa Bay's soft sandy shores or embark on a day trip to St. Petersburg or Sarasota. Now that you have explored the pages of this guide, the only thing left to do is experience Tampa for yourself. This city, with its endless possibilities, is waiting to welcome you, to surprise you, to inspire you, and to create memories that will stay with you long after you leave. Every traveler leaves a piece of themselves in Tampa, and in return, Tampa leaves its mark on them. So, book that flight, pack your bags, and step into a city that promises adventure, beauty, and unforgettable moments. Tampa is more than a destination—it is a feeling, a story waiting to be written, and an experience that will stay in your heart forever.